SURVIVING
FRIENDLY
FIRE

SURVIVING FRIENDLY

FIRE

How to Respond When You're Hurt by Someone You Trust

RON DUNN

THOMAS NELSON PUBLISHERS®
Nashville
A Division of Thomas Nelson, Inc.
www.ThomasNelson.com

Published in Nashville, Tennessee, by Thomas Nelson, Inc.

Unless otherwise noted, Scripture quotations are from the HOLY BIBLE: NEW INTERNATIONAL VERSION®. Copyright © 1973, 1978, 1984 by International Bible Society. Used by permission of Zondervan Publishing House. All rights reserved.

Scripture quotations noted KJV are from the King James Version.

Scripture quotations noted NKJV are from THE NEW KING JAMES VERSION. Copyright © 1979, 1980, 1982 by Thomas Nelson, Inc. Used by permission. All rights reserved.

Scripture quotations noted PHILLIPS are from J. B. Phillips: THE NEW TESTAMENT IN ENGLISH, Revised Edition. Copyright © J. B. Phillips 1958, 1960, 1972. Used by permission of Macmillan Publishing Co., Inc.

Scripture quotations noted WILLIAMS are from the Charles B. Williams translation of the New Testament, copyright © 1986 by Holman Bible Publishers, Nashville, TN.

Scripture quotations noted NASB are from the NEW AMERICAN STANDARD BIBLE®, © Copyright The Lockman Foundation 1960, 1962, 1963, 1968, 1971, 1972, 1975, 1977. Used by permission. <www.Lockman.org>

Scripture quotations noted NRSV are from the NEW REVISED STANDARD VERSION of the Bible. Copyright © 1989 by the Division of Christian Education of the National Council of The Churches of Christ in the U.S.A. All rights reserved.

Library of Congress Cataloging-in-Publication Data

Dunn, Ronald, 1936–2001.
    Surviving friendly fire : how to respond when you're hurt by someone you
  trust / Ronald
Dunn.
      p. cm.
     ISBN 0-7852-6638-0
     1. Friendship—Religious aspects—Christianity. 2. Disappointment—
Religious aspects—Christianity. I. Dunn, Ronald. II. Title.
     BV4647.F7 D86 2001
     241'.6762—dc21   200104274
                                           CIP

Printed in the United States of America

01 02 03 04 05 PHX 5 4 3 2 1

For
Barry and Janet

Sometimes it takes more than a little grease.

CONTENTS

CONTENTS

PROLOGUE

It had never happened before in U.S. military history.

But it was happening to Captain Jim Wang.

He was being court-martialed for twenty-six friendly fire deaths.

Time magazine recorded the incident:

As the two helicopters sliced through the blue skies over northern Iraq last Thursday, a U.S. Air Force AWACS reconnaissance plane picked them up on radar. The AWACS crew immediately radioed a pair of U.S. F-15C fighters and asked them to take a closer look. Though there had been no reported violations of the no-fly zone over northern Iraq since January 1993, Iraqi helicopters had been a problem in the past, when Saddam Hussein used them to suppress the Kurdish rebellion that erupted after the Gulf War ended in 1991. The crews of the F-15Cs twice flew past the copters and identified them as Russian-made Hinds flown by the Iraqi military. The fateful, terse order came back from the AWACS to fire. Moments later, the blasted helicopters, each of them struck by an air-to-air missile, plummeted to the ground.

As horrified Pentagon officials quickly discovered, however, the two choppers were not Hinds but U.S. Black Hawks. On board were 26 allied military and civilian officials . . . The accident virtually wiped out the leadership of the allied Military Coordination Center.

The magazine went on to say that "lives lost to friendly fire are a devastating cost of battle. Almost one-fourth of the 148 American combat deaths in the Gulf War resulted from accidental assault by their own side. The Pentagon established a Fratricide Task Force to develop ways to avoid such accidents."[1] Of the six air force officers investigated, only Captain Wang was court-martialed. He was acquitted of all charges on June 20, 1995.

Friendly fire has always been a feared reality in combat. One official stated that if the truth were known, the number of friendly fire incidents would probably be ten times more than the usual 2 percent estimate.

Never having lost a loved one in combat, I can only imagine the heart-rending grief such a death would inflict. But to learn that your loved one was killed by one of his own would, it seems to me, magnify the pain, now joined by rage, a thousand times over.

But the tragedy of friendly fire is not confined to military combat zones. Whatever we choose to call it, all of us have been wounded by friendly fire. As Lewis Smedes says, "If you live long enough, chances are you'll be hurt by someone you counted on to be your friend . . . When we invest ourselves in deep personal relationships, we open our souls to the wounds of another's disloyalty or even betrayal."[2]

For the past twenty-two years I have held conferences in forty or more churches a year—that's nearly a thousand churches, big and little, city and rural, of this denomination or that—and I have found churches full of wounded and hurting people. It may have been yesterday or a lifetime ago, but it still ulcerates the heart and mind. And what makes this so depressingly tragic is that these wounds have come not from enemies, but from friends. We expect our enemies to hurt us, but when the hurt comes from a friend or a loved one or a trusted one, a pastor or parishioner, a husband or wife, a parent or child, who can measure how deeply that wound buries itself in the soul?

During a conference, a woman shared with me a disturbing problem in her life. I suggested she talk to her pastor about the matter.

She huffed and said, "The last time I told him anything, I ended up as next Sunday's sermon illustration."

Increasing numbers of people tell me that they are reluctant or even refuse to share their hurts with their church friends or church leaders. Philip Yancey reminds us that when Jesus was on earth, troubled people ran to Him to find refuge; now they seem to be running from Him or, rather, from His church. What has happened?[3]

Perhaps you have been wounded by friendly fire, hurt by a friend, betrayed by someone you trusted, let down by someone you depended upon. Maybe the wound was so deep, you have decided to build walls around yourself to ensure that it never happens again. You may feel like a friend of mine who, after a messy divorce, said, "I'll never love anyone again. It hurts too much." After all, if you don't love anyone or trust anybody, how can you be hurt again?

You may have abandoned the church altogether because of the undeserved hurts you received there. But something is missing from your life. The anger is a poor substitute for the peace you once felt; the loneliness of spirit is too high a price to pay for the fellowship of the saints. Perhaps you feel like David when he said out of deep depression,

> These things I remember
>> as I pour out my soul:
> how I used to go with the multitude,
>> leading the procession to the house of God,
> with shouts of joy and thanksgiving
>> among the festive throng. (Ps. 42:4)

The prodigal son's memory of how great things were in his father's house prompted his decision to return home. Do you remember?

I hope that what I say in this book will help you recover from any wounds and heal the painful memories. In Part 1, I deal with being wounded by friendly fire: what it is, what it looks like, and why people do it. Part 2 discusses some biblical ways of surviving friendly fire, and Part 3 is devoted to returning friendly fire—getting even God's way.

PART 1

WOUNDED BY FRIENDLY FIRE

*Histories are more full of examples of the fidelity
of dogs than of friends.*
—ALEXANDER POPE

*We wait in ambush for the novel that fails, for the poet who
commits suicide, for the financier who is a crook, for the
politician who slips, for the priest who is discovered to be
an adulterer. We live in ambush for them all so that we
may gloat at their misfortunes . . . we feel cheated by our
newspapers and magazines if no one is leveled in the
dust in them.*
—HENRY FAIRLIE, British journalist

CHAPTER 1

FRIENDLY FIRE

What is friendly fire?

During a fellowship period after a service one night, two women sat down next to me. "Tell him!" one woman said to the other, a large woman with pain engraved on her face. Shuddering like a child being force-fed broccoli, she began sobbing. Haltingly she told me her story. She and her family belonged to another church in town, a totalitarian church with a dictatorial pastor who taught that every minutia of the church members' lives should be under the authority of the church (the pastor and elders). Her husband was gung ho about this concept and treated his wife as a slave and severely abused her. Finally she could take it no longer and went to one of the elders for help. "Have you ever considered," he asked, "that you might be mentally ill?"

That evening, expecting some semblance of sympathy, she told her husband of her encounter with the elder. The husband looked at her and said, "You might think seriously about that." Later that evening, she overheard her husband calling the elder to thank him for what he said to his wife.

"I don't believe in divorce," she told me in a defeated voice, "so I've stayed with him. I've gained a hundred pounds."

That's friendly fire.

I have a friend who a number of years ago started a street ministry in a large city in Texas. He was (and is) the kind of guy who wasn't afraid to get down and get dirty with the helpless and hopeless teenage derelicts in the gutters of the pitiless city. Runaways, druggies, alcoholics, and gang members were his congregation. God blessed that ministry with many conversions to Christ. He incorporated the ministry and selected trusted friends as board members. Then he met a man truly on the skids. Once a song leader for a then famous evangelist, he had lost everything because of alcohol. My friend gave him a car, helped him buy a home, gave him thousands of dollars to get back on his feet, and hired him as a fund-raiser for the growing ministry.

My friend, a high-energy person and tireless worker, eventually pushed himself to the point of exhaustion and was hospitalized. While he was in the hospital, the man he helped never visited him; he was busy convincing the board members he could run the ministry better than my friend. Some board members resigned; others stayed on and, under the persuasion of this man, "retired" my friend. His ministry was stolen from him by a man he had befriended and trusted.

That's friendly fire.

The Bible is full of instances of friendly fire: Cain slaying his brother, Abel; Jacob stealing the birthright from his brother, Esau; Joseph betrayed by his brothers; Peter forsaking Jesus; Paul abandoned by his brethren while he was in prison.

WHY FRIENDLY FIRE?

In trying to understand how these and contemporary Christians could lie, deceive, and betray their fellow believers, I came to a conclusion. Before this kind of malicious behavior can live in a person, something must first die in that person.

THE DEATH OF INTEGRITY AND OTHER GOOD THINGS

We read in Proverbs: "The integrity of the upright guides them, but the unfaithful are destroyed by their duplicity" (11:3).

Everyone seems to be talking about integrity these days, specifically its loss. I think most people would agree that one of the greatest failures, especially among leaders, more especially among politicians, is the failure of integrity.

Stephen Carter, in his book *Integrity*, maintains that this is perhaps "first among the virtues that make for a good character because that in some sense it is prior to everything else: the rest of what we think matters very little if we lack essential integrity, the courage of our convictions, the willingness to act and speak in behalf of what we know is right."[1] The French dramatist Jean Baptiste Molière stated, "If everyone were clothed with integrity, if every heart were just, kindly, the other virtues would be well-nigh useless, since their chief purpose is to make us bear with patience the injustice of our fellows." These comments apply to the offender and the offended.

The idea of the word *integrity*, quoted in the verse from Proverbs, is wholeness, completeness, an undivided mind and heart. Jesus said, "Blessed are the pure in heart: for they shall see God" (Matt. 5:8 KJV); *pure* meaning "unmixed, unadulterated, unalloyed." Barclay translates it: "Blessed is the man whose motives are always entirely unmixed, for that man shall see God."[2] The author of Proverbs contrasted the integrity of the upright with the *duplicity* of the unfaithful. Duplicity—twisting words, talking out of both sides of the mouth, saying one thing and doing another—will destroy the unfaithful. But integrity—discerning what is right from wrong and acting on that knowledge, committed wholly to God's will and behaving in harmony with that will—will guide the upright to the right course of action.

A person of integrity believes in virtues rather than values. Have you noticed lately that everyone talks about values, but the word *virtue* is almost extinct in our vocabulary, like an old car rusting in a junkyard? In the 1880s the German agnostic philosopher Friedrich Nietzsche began to speak of values denoting the moral beliefs and attitudes of a society. In his thinking (by the way, Nietzsche and sociologist Max Weber laid the foundation for much of the way people think today) there is no good or evil, no virtue or vice; there exist only values.

So what's the big deal?

Values assume that all moral ideas are subjective and relative, mere customs and conventions. Gertrude Himmelfarb, in her book *The De-Moralization of Society*, writes, "Values, as we now understand that word, do not have to be virtues; they can be beliefs, opinions, attitudes, feelings, habits, conventions, preferences . . . whatever any individual, group, or society happens to value, at any time, for any reason."[3]

That is why it is unpopular today to say that someone is right or wrong; each person must make up his own mind according to his likes and dislikes. Virtues are absolute; values are relative. When virtues were still legal tender, people believed "that they were the standards against which all behavior could and should be measured. The standards were firm even if the behavior of individuals did not always measure up to them. And when conduct fell short of those standards, it was judged in moral terms, as bad, wrong, or evil—not as . . . misguided, undesirable or (the most recent corruption of our moral vocabulary) 'inappropriate.'"[4]

A person of integrity believes that there are standards against which behavior can and should be measured, even if sticking to those standards costs him personally. A man of integrity is someone we can trust to keep his word, to tell the truth, and to act in fairness, both in word and in deed. God had integrity in mind when in Psalm 15, He described the true believer, the one after His own heart:

O LORD, who may abide in Thy tent?
Who may dwell on Thy holy hill?

He who walks with integrity, and works righteousness,
And speaks truth in his heart.
He does not slander with his tongue,
Nor does evil to his neighbor,
Nor takes up a reproach against his friend;
In whose eyes a reprobate is despised,
But who honors those who fear the LORD;
He swears to his own hurt, and does not change;
He does not put out his money at interest
[doesn't take advantage of another's problems],
Nor does he take a bribe against the innocent.
He who does these things will never be shaken. (NASB)

The phrase "swears to his own hurt, and does not change" catches my attention. I spoke earlier of the fact that integrity may cost us personally. A person makes a promise to a friend but later finds that keeping the promise will work to his disadvantage, "to his own hurt." What does he do? He keeps his word, as the psalmist said.

When I was in seminary, my wife and I bought a little house from a friend who had just graduated. We lived there a couple of years, then moved to a church about thirty miles away. A close friend said he wanted to buy the house as an investment. We agreed on details and on the day we would finalize the transaction. On the day agreed, I showed up on his doorstep. My friend opened the door and, from behind the screen door, told me he had changed his mind. And that was it. To be true, I would have released him from his promise if he had asked. But he never contacted me and asked about it. He waited until I arrived at his doorstep. He swore to his own hurt—and changed. It was embarrassing to me because my father was with me; it put us in a bind for a while, but we recovered. The problem is that whenever I think of my friend, I never remember all the good times we had together—I remember only the day he broke his word. Maybe I need to read this book.

The death of integrity also brings about the death of *duty*, *honor*, and *loyalty*, which are active ingredients of integrity.

For Christians, the death of integrity must also mean the death of the *unity of the community*. Sad to say, life in community exposes us to friendly fire. L. Gregory Jones comments, "The 'deepest truth' about ourselves . . . is that we are created for communion with God, with one another, and with the whole creation."[5] God wants to live in communion with us and so created us in His image and likeness. Rather than being created to live an isolated, individual life, we were made to live in fellowship with God and one another. It is only by living in this communion that we fulfill our God-given purpose and destiny.

GOD'S ORIGINAL INTENTION

God's original intention was that the world, His creation, live in fellowship with Him and one another. That's why He created us in His image. But the world failed. Man disobeyed God, breaking that fellowship with Him, then brother killed brother, breaking fellowship with one another.

But then God made another creation—the church. This new creation was to fulfill the intentions of the old creation. The church is supposed to be a microcosm of what the world should be. But we, too, have failed.

John made it clear that fellowship with Christ and fellowship with one another are intertwined (1 John 1:3–7). We can't have one without the other. We cannot remain in fellowship with Christ if we are not in fellowship with one another. We must, therefore, maintain our fellowship with one another if there is to be fellowship with Christ. We can't be right with God and wrong with our neighbors.

In his book *Life Together*, Dietrich Bonhoeffer writes, "Christian brotherhood is not an ideal which we must realize; it is rather a reality created by God in Christ in which we may participate. The more clearly we learn to recognize that the ground and strength and promise of all our fellowship is in Jesus Christ, the more serenely shall we think of our fellowship and pray and hope for it."[6] This truth should do away with all selfish and petty desires. It should be the death knell of gossip, slander, and backbiting—the end of friendly fire. The person who engages in unity-threatening behavior is ignorant of this truth or has subverted it to his selfish goals, an individual obsessed with his personal agenda.

I talked with a young man about his experiences with Alcoholics Anonymous and Narcotics Anonymous. He had nothing but good things to say about the programs. "There," he said, "I'm able to just be myself and share my problems." Knowing he was a church member, I asked him if he had shared any of his problems with the church.

"Absolutely not!" he exclaimed.

When I asked him why, he said, "In AA and NA, I know that whatever I say will be met with understanding and compassion. The people in the church would just condemn me."

Paul insisted that "each of you must put off falsehood and speak truthfully to his neighbor." Why? *For we are all members of one body*" (Eph. 4:25, emphasis added). Therefore, he added, "Do not let any unwholesome talk come out of your mouths, but only what is helpful for building others up" (v. 29). But instead many churches are like the Galatians, whom Paul described as "biting and devouring each other" (Gal. 5:15).

Larry Crabb writes, "The greatest need in modern civilization is the development of communities—true communities where the heart of God is home, where the humble and wise learn to shepherd those on the path behind them, where trusting strugglers lock arms with others as together they journey on."[7]

WHAT DOES FRIENDLY FIRE LOOK LIKE?

A young couple in our church felt God's call to be missionaries in Hong Kong. After enduring the pains and strains of missionary preparation, they finally began their ministry in

Hong Kong. They loved it and developed a highly productive work there until, after four years, they were sent home on furlough. Nothing was said by the administration to prepare them for what was about to occur. One day, during their furlough, they received word that they would not be allowed to return to Hong Kong. The news was devastating to the young missionary couple, for they had planted their hearts in the then British Crown Colony. They had started a work. What would become of it? No sensible reason was given, except the feeble explanation that they had not "adjusted to the foreign." Dozens of letters of protest and recommendations were written to the board. All futile. Several years later, they were told, "It was all politics; you should never have been returned to the U.S."

A couple spent years as members of the same church— from the time they were married until they became senior adults. They served in numerous capacities of leadership during those years. It was his tireless and selfless work that kept the church on course at several critical points. They were among the most faithful members of the congregation. The pastor had remarked on several occasions that if they ever left the church, he was going with them. Then came retirement when they were ready to devote themselves full-time to the church. Imagine the wounds inflicted upon them when new leadership made it clear it was not interested in "old people." All those years of devoted service and hard-earned experience discarded because of a different approach to ministry.

Friendly fire can come from a variety of sources, inflicting invisible wounds that breed invisible tears—invisible to others, and sometimes, through denial, invisible to us.

But remember this: friendly fire need not be fatal. You can survive it; God has made ample provisions to carry you through to healing and victory. And these are the things we're going to explore in this book.

"Man is born to trouble," said Job, "as surely as sparks fly upward" (Job 5:7). Before we get into the details of friendly fire, its *hows* and *whys*, I think it would be helpful to discuss in a general way the emotional hurts we all receive on the path of our existence.

CHAPTER 2

WHERE IS EVERYBODY?

If I were Jesus (I speak as a fool), I think the most disappointing day of my life would have been resurrection day.

Why?

Because not a single person was there to welcome Him back from the dead—none of His disciples, none of His friends. It wasn't that they were uninformed. Jesus had repeatedly told them that He would rise on the third day. They were in hiding, huddled together around their fear and faithlessness, and missed the dawning of a new world.

But I doubt that Jesus was surprised at their absence. After all, they had forsaken Him during His hours of greatest need, the hours of His passion. Peter had bragged that he was ready to go to prison with Him and even to die with Him. Empty words from an arrogant heart. At a time when they should have gathered around Him, offering comfort and companionship, the disciples were fighting over who was the greatest (Luke 22:24). Like children arguing over who's going to get the silverware while the mother lies dying in the next room, they were debating who should take over leadership when Jesus was gone.

At the beginning of Part 1, I quoted Alexander Pope, who said, "Histories are more full of examples of the fidelity of dogs than of friends." I wonder what betrayals he suffered to cause him to say that.

A VIEW FROM THE PIT

Maybe he had some friends like those of Paul. In 2 Timothy, the apostle wrote his last letter from prison. In the fourth chapter he spoke of those who abandoned him at his great hour of need. "Demas," he said, "because he loved this world, has deserted me" (4:10). The Greek word means "to be left in the lurch." He encouraged Timothy to come as soon as possible and to bring his cloak and his scrolls, especially the parchments.

Paul was alone and lonely, like a dying soldier lying forgotten on an empty battlefield. According to John Stott, Paul was lonely, cold, and bored.[1] And then when he was taken from that dark, damp dungeon to appear before the court for his preliminary hearing, he said, "At my first defense, no one came to my support, but everyone deserted me" (4:16). I guess all those fine Roman Christians found it more convenient to be elsewhere that day. But Paul discovered what he already knew and what we know—people are fickle.

I hate to admit it, but preachers know this all too well. That's where the expression "Christians shoot their wounded" came from. People want to be on the side of the winners, the popular, and the praised. When a pastor finds himself in trouble, whether it's his doing or not, he often discovers that many he thought were friends were not. He receives few, if any, phone calls of encouragement; no one visits him; his wife and family are ostracized by the very people they once socialized with.

In contrast to this pattern, Paul told us that even if one of our brethren is caught in a sin, "you who are spiritual should restore him gently," and we are to "do good to all people, *especially to those who belong to the family of believers*" (Gal. 6:1, 10, emphasis added).

I recall too many occasions where elderly parents, unable to care for themselves, were literally abandoned like worn-out clothes by their children and the church had to step in and do what their selfish children should have been doing.

I know of Christian parents who, because their son had AIDS, were shunned by their fellow church members and became persona non grata in their own church.

Because of severe physical problems, a pastor's wife was unable to attend church and continually received hate calls from church members, scoffing at her illness and accusing her of deserting the church.

These people have a right to ask, "Where is everybody?"

One of my dearest friends is Dr. Harold O'Chester, pastor of the Great Hills Baptist Church in Austin, Texas. In the sixties, he pastored a church in Mississippi. Here is his story: "On Easter Sunday morning, 1968, the Ku Klux Klan burned the seventh black church in our county. A church member called me crying because her maid had just called, saying, 'They burned my church and it's Easter morning.'

"I scrapped my Easter message and preached to an overflow crowd on justice. When I said I could not live in a community with this kind of hatred, they gave me a standing ovation. The next morning I went to the Chamber of Commerce, and we began the first biracial group of Mississippians since Reconstruction days. Our purpose was to raise money to rebuild these churches.

"The KKK immediately began to discuss what they would do. After several meetings they decided I would be the one they would use to demonstrate to the Mississippi world not to mess with the KKK. They decided to firebomb my house, just as they had the grocery store in Hattiesburg, killing the grocer. That story is told in the movie *Mississippi Burning*.

"The FBI and the local police chief called me to police headquarters to tell me about the Klan's plan. They had an informer inside the Klan. My wife and I and our three daughters left the front bedrooms and slept on the sofas in the den at the back of our house. We were under personal FBI and local police protection for eighty-two days.

"During that time the local Jewish temple was dynamited. A local black businessman and the president of the temple were also targeted. A Jewish man's house was bombed. The assailant was wounded and captured.

"Because of my stand, I began to get national attention

from newspapers and periodicals. The religious editor of *Newsweek* called for an interview. I asked the chairman of our deacons to meet with us so I would have someone to back up my statements to the press in the event they did not quote me correctly.

"When the article came out, it recorded accurately what I had said about the Committee of Conscience, as it was called. There was a picture of me standing in front of one of the burned-out black churches. The last sentence of the article, however, said, without quotes, 'that my next step was the integration of my church.'

"I never said that, and it would have been foolish to do, given the climate in Mississippi at that time. It hit the stands on Thursday, and by Friday several deacons called for my firing (some of them had been Klan members when they were younger).

"They called for a deacons' meeting on Saturday night. The chairman told me of the meeting on Saturday morning. I said to him, 'I see no need for me to be there. You just tell them I never made that statement with regard to integration.'

"He looked at me and said, 'I can't do that.'

"I was amazed and asked why.

"He said, 'You've had five good years here as pastor and can leave anytime you want to, but this is my home, and if I make a statement like that, it will affect my business.'

"I was flabbergasted. I told him that this was a matter of integrity. He knew what had been said and what had not been said.

"But he refused to change his mind, so he said nothing at the meeting. Fortunately cooler heads prevailed, and even though six deacons voted to fire me, fifteen voted no. There were five more votes to fire me until they finally gave up. The rejection by that man whom I loved and prayed for hurt me deeply."

It is a sin to abandon a brother or sister in the person's time of need. Notice in 2 Timothy 4:16 where Paul asked God not to hold it against those who deserted him. "Charged to their account" is a better translation. It is a bookkeeping term for charging a bill to someone's account. Even though they might have deserved it, Paul asked God not to charge it against them.

But it is also a sin to be bitter about it. Paul showed us that when he asked God not to hold it against them. That was probably the opposite of what most of us would pray concerning such fickle folk.

From his view from the pit, Paul discovered something else—although people may be fickle, the Lord is faithful. He said, "But the Lord stood at my side and gave me strength" (4:17). The Lord stood by him, the word *stood* being used in those days of a legal adviser who stood by the defendant and whispered advice to him. Everyone else may forsake us, but the Lord stands by us and speaks to us. He comes to our defense; He *is* our defense.

> The soul that on Jesus hath leaned for repose
> I will not, I will not desert to his foes;

That soul, tho' all hell should endeavor to shake,
I'll never, no, never, no, never forsake.[2]

The Lord is faithful. In closing this passage, Paul declared, "The Lord will rescue me from every evil attack and will bring me safely to his heavenly kingdom" (4:18). The Lord will rescue me from every evil attack? Well, Paul missed it there, I guess, because he was shortly executed. No, he didn't miss it. If his execution had been an evil thing, the Lord would have rescued him from it. Paul's death was, to him, not an evil work because it ushered him into the presence of Jesus where for years he had longed to be. Rest assured, if the Lord doesn't deliver you from something "evil," it must not be evil for you. This same paradox appears in 1 Peter 3:13–14, where Peter was dealing with the persecution of believers and yet said, "Who is going to harm you if you are eager to do good? But even if you should suffer for what is right, you are blessed." Only believers can appreciate and experience this strange doctrine.

TURNING YOUR PIT INTO A PULPIT

As a matter of fact, such suffering enables you to turn your pit into a pulpit, as it did with Paul. Describing his absence of friends and the presence of the Lord who stood by him and strengthened him, he said, "So that through me the message might be fully proclaimed and all the Gentiles might hear it" (2 Tim. 4:17). That was Paul's original commission—to take

19

the message of Christ to the Gentiles, and his terrible and traumatic experience enabled him to fulfill the will of God for his life. In the same way, nothing speaks louder and clearer of the sufficiency of God's grace than the trustful way we react in similar situations.

Therefore, Paul concluded with a doxology: "To him be glory for ever and ever. Amen" (4:18). When we come to know the adequacy of His presence, we will be able to move through life with a doxology on our lips.

> Yes, Thou art ever present, Power Supreme!
> Not circumscribed by Time, nor fixed to Space,
> Confined to altars, nor to temples bound,
> In Wealth, in Want, in Freedom or in Chains,
> In Dungeons or on Thrones, the faithful find Thee!
>
> (HANNAH MORE)

CHAPTER 3

INVISIBLE TEARS

The violation of personhood begins in the cradle, if not in the womb.

—Theodore Rosak

She was leaning against the wall in the auditorium, her body racked with uncontrollable weeping. It seemed the twenty-year-old woman just couldn't get assurance that God had forgiven her sin. Her friends asked me to talk to her.

When she told me that she didn't believe God could forgive her, I said, "You need to see God as a Father who loves . . ."

Suddenly she shoved me back and cried out, "Don't use the word *father* to me!"

Bewildered, I asked what she meant. In between heavy sobs, she related to me the years of abuse she had suffered from her father. The visible tears of God's unforgiveness were a subterfuge for the invisible tears of her father's abuse.

TRAGEDY AND TRAUMA

Her story tells of a double tragedy. First, this loathsome betrayal came from one whom she loved and trusted, one whose sole goal in life should have been to care for, nurture, and protect her: her father. Second, the trauma from the tragedy has endured into her adult life, inflicting upon her invisible tears that may never dry up. For her father the bestial incidents lasted only a few grunting moments, but for her each traitorous second was a forever.

Dr. Bruce Perry, through his research at CIVITAS Child Trauma Programs, believes that trauma inflicted upon children leaves physical markers spotted as easily as footprints in the snow. The effects of abuse, neglect, and domestic violence show up in heart rates that alternately race and plummet; in stiffened muscles and low-grade fevers; in difficulty in learning, sleeping, or just standing still. Perry says these altered states can become enduring, even permanent, traits.[1]

But evidence shows that the trauma inflicted by friendly fire can reach back farther than childhood, even in the womb or at birth. Indeed, the first experiences of emotional shock usually occur in the first few months of life and even before birth. David Brenner writes,

> The developing fetus is capable of experiencing emotional trauma and of retaining the effects of this trauma after birth. Psychologists interested in these prenatal emotional wounds suggest that such things as an unsuccessful

attempt at induced abortion or even the experience of residing within the womb of a woman who deeply resents the pregnancy may be emotionally traumatic for the fetus and may produce psychological consequences not unlike those associated with postnatal emotional trauma . . . The birth process itself can sometimes have negative emotional consequences; some problems in adulthood seem to be best understood as originating in a protracted or difficult birth.[2]

I have on my desk a letter from a friend whose nephew could not overcome his stuttering. At age fifteen, under deep hypnosis, he told the doctor that when he was about twelve months old, he remembered standing in his crib watching his father hit his mother. When the doctor related this to the mother, she confirmed that it had happened exactly as her son described.

For years many have looked upon hypnosis with great suspicion. But in the last generation, many doctors have found it to be a valid tool in helping certain patients. I took a minor in psychology at my university and found that, in most instances, hypnosis proves to be a valuable tool.

Another patient, a state senator, trying to recover from stuttering, related the event of his birth. Again, under deep hypnosis, he described how the doctor was not ready for the birth, became very agitated, was not gentle, and cursed during the entire procedure. After the senator came out from under hypnosis, the doctor told him what he had said. The patient had no memory of it. But when he discussed it with his mother, she confirmed the whole episode, saying she had never spoken of it to her son.

THE HURT GOES ON

Growing up is tough. Parents can be insensitive, negligent, even abusive.

Teachers can be prejudiced. Other children can be cruel—and too often are. "Perhaps the first moral judgment uttered by a young child is, 'That's not fair.'"[3] Walter Wangerin Jr. says that as good parents, we try to teach our children to be fair: "All we teach them is based upon the presumption that there is a reasonable law at work in the world—reasonable and feasible and universal and impartial: *The Law of Fairness*."[4] This belief in the law of fairness is one of the first casualties of our encounter with the world. All too soon we learn that the world doesn't operate according to the law of fairness. The law of the world is *the law of selfishness*. And this law can be satisfied only by breaking the law of fairness. Selfishness can obtain its goal only by being unfair, unkind, unloving, and insensitive.

The taunts of the playground, the shove by the school bully, the twitting laughter, the public humiliation by a teacher—in the memory they gain tenure and torture us even into adulthood. All of us can remember such acts of unfairness and hurt that reduced our self-esteem and self-confidence and that, more than likely, were downplayed by our parents if we reported our injuries to them at all. But memory doesn't downplay even the slightest hurt; it sharpens itself like a pencil and writes our dreams. The past keeps happening.

. . . AND ON

The teenage years. Years that are delicious and terrible, happy and miserable, a body undergoing mysterious and magical changes, a body growing out of control, growing faster than the emotions, trapped in that no-man's-land between childhood and adulthood—too old to be a child, too young to be an adult, with a psyche screaming for approval, affirmation, and acceptance. A time of great expectations.

These vulnerable growing-up years provide easy opportunities for being wounded. A twelve-year-old girl in our church had what every kid wishes she had: parents with no rules. This child could go where she wanted to, when she wanted to, stay out as late as she wanted to, and her parents never questioned her. There were no guidelines. Every kid's dream, right? But she sat in my office in tears, saying her parents cared nothing for her, a conclusion based on her parents' seeming indifference to what she did, like unclaimed baggage at an airport. "If they loved me," she said, "they would care what I did." Constantly clamoring for attention, she took to fainting regularly while I was preaching, bringing the service to a grinding halt while people rushed to her aid. She simply wanted someone to worry about her. She certainly got my attention.

We parents often think, mistakenly, that our children are extensions of ourselves—that they will be like us, think like us, work like us, have convictions like ours. When we forget that we have given birth to a life, a separate life, a whole other individual, who must become his own person, we burden our children with exacting demands. Then, when they don't measure up, we tend to ridicule and put them down.

"I wish you had never been born!" (That makes two of us.)
"Why can't you be more like your brother?" (I hate him.)
"Can't you do anything right?" (I try; I really do.)
"You'll never amount to anything!" (Thanks.)

These barbs are flung out of the frustration of overloaded parents. They rarely mean what they say. And sad to say, they rarely correct themselves, leaving the child with a sense of betrayal and worthlessness. Instead of being encouraging and affirming, such parents are about as comforting as a parka in the middle of August. A parent is the fool of all fools if he doesn't think these (to him, harmless) put-downs and asides have a negative effect on the child's sense of self-worth and may well define the paths taken throughout the rest of life. In the novel *The God of Small Things*, Arundhati Roy's heroine, Rahel, a small child, does something that angers her mother. In response, her mother says, "When you do something like that it makes people love you less." The phrase "loves you less" fastens itself to Rahel's mind like a parasite, and throughout the rest of her childhood, she is devoured by the conviction that her mother loves her less.

One of the most painful wounds a child can receive is the loss, either by death or by divorce, of a parent. Usually the younger the child at the time of the loss, the more devastating the effect. Such a loss is one of the most intensely painful experiences a human being can suffer because a child's first human relationship is the foundation stone of his personality.[5] Whatever happens in your family shapes your personality and behavior. Monica McGoldrich writes, "Unfortunately it is not possible to destroy our history. It lives on inside, probably the more powerful for our attempts to bury it. We and our families are likely to pay a high price in the present for trying to block out the past."[6] According to the 1990 census, more than 873,000 American girls, eighteen years and younger, were living with their single fathers. "Of all children raised in single-parent homes, these girls may have the most personal difficulty in later life."[7]

Conversely David Blankenhorn laments that the United States is becoming an increasingly fatherless society: "Never before in this country have so many children been voluntarily abandoned by their fathers. Never before have so many children grown up without knowing what it means to have a father . . . Fatherlessness is the most harmful demographic trend of this generation. It is the leading cause of declining child well-being in our society."[8]

Another source of childhood trauma that is receiving much attention nowadays is the subject of abuse, physical and sexual. A 1984 report (*Sexual Offenses Against Children*) of the minister of justice and the attorney general of Canada stated that a study of ten thousand cases of childhood sexual abuse suggested that between 20 and 40 percent of females and between 10 and 25 percent of males are victims of sexual abuse in the childhood years. Sexually abused children experience short-term and long-term emotional and personality disorders, most of whom never receive professional help and emerge into adulthood with traumatic consequences. It is impossible to measure the disastrous impact of such an experience on a child.

Unfortunately all the attention to childhood sexual abuse has spawned another evil hurt—the false memory syndrome. Jumping on the bandwagon of childhood sexual abuse, some therapists have devoted their entire practice to uncovering repressed memories of sexual abuse. After gaining a patient's confidence, the therapist presents him with a list of symptoms. If the patient has experienced, in some cases, even one of these symptoms, the therapist tells him that he was sexually abused as a child. And if the patient doesn't recall such an incident, the therapist explains that he is repressing the memory. He was sexually abused even if he can't remember it. In many instances erroneous lawsuits have been filed against the "offending" father and/or mother. While many reports of incest and sexual abuse are true, many are the results of a therapy-induced false memory, causing wrongful imprisonment, separation of families, and parental anguish that often ends in divorce. The False Memory Center of Philadelphia has on record a staggering thirteen thousand cases of false memory accusations.[9]

AND THE SPARKS KEEP FLYING UPWARD

Like most teenagers, I lived those years like a sprinter, straining everything within me to break through the tape to adulthood. Hooray for adulthood! If I could just hang on until I reached that blessed milestone, everything would be okay. Out of school, out from under my parents' thumb, out of the home and on my own, then I could run my life my way, the right way. Like the Israelites at the Red Sea, who thought the Egyptians were their only enemies, not realizing that on the other side waited the Canaanites, the Hittites, and all the other -ites, I didn't know that crossing over into adulthood would bring its own set of troubles.

But man is born to trouble. Bills. Income tax. Victim of downsizing. An unfaithful spouse. Children who break your heart and keep you awake all night. A failed romance. A friend criticizing you behind your back. A husband forgetting his wife's birthday or their anniversary. And as we grow older, the issues become more serious. When I was a teenager, it was pimples. Now it's tumors, and I'm sometimes tempted to warn kids against growing up. There's no getting around it. From the cradle to the grave we are vulnerable to the undeserved hurts rendered by others.

BUT MUST THE PAST DETERMINE
THE PRESENT?

I have some good news for all who have been hurt. Past hurts need not rule your present or future happiness. Salvation is available; deliverance is within your reach—or more precisely in the reach of Christ.

In Colossians 1:16–18, speaking of Christ, Paul said, "For by him all things were created: things in heaven and on earth, visible and invisible, *whether thrones or powers or rulers or authorities*; all things were created by him and for him . . . so that in everything he might have the supremacy" (emphasis added).

And in Colossians 2, writing of Christ's victory on the cross, he wrote, "And having disarmed *the powers and authorities*, he made a public spectacle of them, triumphing over them by the cross" (v. 15, emphasis added).

In Ephesians 6, Paul told us that we struggle *"against the rulers, against the authorities, against the powers of this dark world and against the spiritual forces of evil in the heavenly realms"* (v. 12, emphasis added).

In these passages, when Paul spoke of *rulers* and *powers* and *authorities*, he was referring to the dark powers of evil and demonic forces. These are the invisible forces that seek to determine our destiny. And Paul stated that we struggle (wrestle, engage in hand-to-hand combat) against these forces. The world tells us that our lives are determined by heredity, environment, natural and social and economic forces over which we have no control. But Christ battled those supernatural forces that enslaved the human race. He conquered them, stripped them of their armor, then exposed them.

You may say you're an abusive parent because you had abusive parents, or you're an alcoholic because your mother or father was an alcoholic.

Recently a young man was on trial for murder, and his attorney's first line of defense was that he had been abused as a child. I wouldn't dare underestimate the vehement influence of being raised in such an environment. *But your present doesn't have to be enslaved by your past.*

From Paul we learn several potent truths about these hidden forces:

1. Christ is supreme, Lord and Master over them.

2. Christ stripped them of their power to control us by His death on the cross.

3. We overcome these malevolent powers by being strong in the Lord (His strength, not ours) and in His mighty power, clothed in His full armor.

Stay with me, for as we proceed we will learn more and more about surviving friendly fire.

Now let's get down to the specifics of friendly fire and why Christians wound other Christians.

CHAPTER 4

THE HAND OF SAUL

*David sang to the LORD the words of this song when
the LORD delivered him from the hand of all his enemies and from the hand of Saul.*

—2 SAMUEL 22:1

It was a sudden and short friendship. I met him one year at
our annual denominational meeting, and he almost immediately invited me to come to his church the following year for
a series of meetings. It was one of the most significant meetings of my life. God immediately began to teach me things
about the lordship of Christ and the fullness of the Spirit I had
never known. The change that occurred in my life was more
dramatic than my conversion experience. A revival started in
my heart, and I carried it back to my church where God did a
supernatural work. The next year my new friend came to my
church, and it was one of the most awesome works of God our
people had witnessed.

We invited him back the next year, anticipating what

would happen. And something did happen. My friend turned against me.

My secretary picked him up at the airport. Barely was he in the car before the air was charged with innuendos about me and my ministry. He insinuated that the church was going downhill and that I was looking for a greener pastorate. My secretary was flabbergasted. She knew that the church was growing as never before and attendance was at an all-time high—as were the budget and the harmony of the fellowship. She also knew that I did not have the slightest desire to leave.

During the week, he would ask to listen to my taped messages, and then in the following service, without referring to me, of course, he would challenge whatever I had preached on the tape. After the services he would bird-dog members to their cars, asking what was wrong with their pastor. Did he seem to be cold and totally out of the meeting?

But my people picked up on the veiled accusations. My deacons asked me to send him packing. I caught my staff in a secret meeting, discussing what they could do to protect me.

When the longest week I think I've known was over, he returned to his church and told them in a public service that I had killed the meeting, that our church was dying and I was backslidden. We have talked several times since then about that meeting, and he feigns ignorance about it all. To this day I do not understand why he betrayed me, though I do have some thoughts.

Instead of discrediting me as he hoped, however, the church gathered around me in exuberant and abundant support. The Lord had delivered me "from the hand of Saul." A fellow pastor pointed out to me the significance of the verse that heads this chapter. David made a distinction between being delivered from the hand of his enemies and from the hand of Saul. His enemies I can understand, but Saul? David and King Saul were citizens of the same nation, served the same God, fought for the same causes, were on the same side.

Saul's story is a sad one. When Saul attacked the Amalekites, he was supposed to take the king and all their livestock and sacrifice them to the Lord. But Saul decided to sacrifice only the worthless livestock, keeping the best and the king for himself. When Samuel confronted him with his disobedience, the prophet declared that the Lord had rejected Saul as king over Israel. Saul's grief at that declaration threw him into deep depression. Upon advice from his counselors, he had David brought to him to sing and play his harp until the depression left. Saul told David's father, Jesse, that he wanted David to remain with him in his service: "Allow David to remain in my service, *for I am pleased with him*" (1 Sam. 16:22, emphasis added).

And yet Saul spent much of his remaining reign trying to destroy the sweet singer of Israel. Why?

THE SPEAR-THROWERS

What character deficiencies must a person possess who slings arrows and darts at his friends?

JEALOUSY

Whatever Saul told David to do, David did it successfully. So successful was David that after he had killed the Philistine and the army returned home, the women from all the towns of Israel crowded the streets singing this song: "Saul has slain his thousands, and David his tens of thousands" (1 Sam. 18:7).

This little refrain so galled and angered Saul that he was suddenly consumed with jealousy: "And from that time on Saul kept a jealous eye on David . . . When Saul saw how successful [David] was, he was afraid of him" (vv. 9, 15). Nothing is as frightening to a jealous man as to hear praises of the person he envies. That was when Saul tried to pin David to the wall with a spear. Saul was possessed with the green-eyed demon. It's a story as old as Cain, who killed his brother, Abel, out of jealousy.

In 1 Samuel 13:3–4 we read, "Jonathan attacked the Philistine outpost at Geba, and the Philistines heard about it. Then Saul had the trumpet blown throughout the land and said, 'Let the Hebrews hear!' So all Israel heard the news: 'Saul has attacked the Philistine outpost.'" Saul, why did you feel the need to take credit for Jonathan's victory? Were you jealous of your own son? Why did you control the information to the press? Why were you so interested in self-promotion? Was momentary praise worth so many years of heartache and misery?

Fueled by self-love, jealousy robs the mind of clear thinking, burns in the heart, resents another's success, brooks no rival, refuses to let its object out of its sight and, like a thief, lies in wait for the slightest mistake. That's why sometimes the best news we can hear is bad news about another. Second only to that pleasure is the opportunity to spread the bad news.

> And all who told it added something new,
> And all who heard it made enlargements too.
> (ALEXANDER POPE)

MY WAY OR NO WAY

Samuel did as God asked and told Saul to attack the Amalekites: "Now go, attack the Amalekites and totally destroy everything that belongs to them. Do not spare them; put to death men and women, children and infants, cattle and sheep, camels and donkeys" (1 Sam. 15:3). But instead of doing it God's way, Saul spared the king and the best of the sheep and cattle, the fat calves and lambs—everything that was good. "These they were unwilling to destroy completely" (v. 9).

And then when Samuel confronted Saul with his sin, Saul tried to cover up his disobedience. Then the Lord said, "I am grieved that I have made Saul king" (v. 11).

Saul lost a crown, a kingdom, his son, and eventually his life—all because he didn't want to follow God's way. It was his way or no way. As a consequence, he went from "God is with you" to "God is against you."

People with this attitude violate one of the basic concepts

of the Christian life: dying to self. Jesus said, "If anyone would come after me, he must deny himself and take up his cross daily and follow me" (Luke 9:23). I like the way Williams translates it: "If any man chooses to be my disciple, *he must say 'no' to self*" (emphasis added). Does your self ever talk to you? Make suggestions? Do you hear anything like this: "Look out for number one," or "Don't let them get by with that," or "Don't let anyone tell you what to do"? To follow Jesus, you must learn to say no to the suggestions of the flesh and yes to Christ.

Our Lord clearly stated, "The man who loves his life will lose it" (John 12:25). The word translated "life" here is *psyche*, the self, the mind, where decisions are decided and choices made. Christ was speaking of those who love to have their own way, make their own choices, follow their own will. He said this person will "lose" his life. It is a present-tense verb, which indicates he is already "losing it."

The Inuit of Canada and Greenland have an unusual way to hunt bears. They take a piece of wolf bone, sharpen both ends to a point, coil it, and then freeze it in blubber. They place it on the path that bears follow, and then they wait.

After a while a bear waddles down the path, spots the blubber, and swallows it. The moment he swallows it, he has killed himself. Every step, every movement, causes the sharpened bone to slash and cut the stomach of the bear. The Inuit follow the bear, and when he finally collapses from internal bleeding, they pounce upon him. The person who insists on his way or no way is destroying himself with every step he takes.

INSECURITY

Many people experience difficulty in finding themselves in the world. As was said of Willie Loman in *The Death of a Salesman*, "he never knew who he was," hosts of people don't know who or what they are. They are not at peace with themselves. Psychologist Rollo May notes that one of the central problems of modern man is that he sees himself without significance as an individual.[1] In the presence of an increasingly overcrowded world, mushrooming technology that is fast replacing man, and celebrity worship, of which he is not one, he sees himself as impotent and inconsequential.

Like the foolish farmer in Luke 12 who thought that being was having and that heaven could be found in a barn, the insecure person believes that a man's life consists in the abundance of things he possesses. This person, therefore, lives in fear and envy—fear of those who have less (they may steal his stuff) and envy of those who have more.

But the moment he chooses to slander, criticize, and accuse, he is no longer impotent and insignificant. He suddenly becomes a small center of attention. People come to him for the latest scoop. He has power, even though the power is only to destroy and tear down. Many people are empty, insecure, alone; they feel real only when other people listen to them and take notice.

Eric Fromm proposes:

If I am what I have and if what I have is lost, who then am I? Nobody but a defeated, deflated, pathetic testimony to a wrong way of living. Because I *can* lose what I have, I am necessarily constantly worried that I shall *lose* what I have . . .

If I am who I am and not what I have, nobody can deprive me or threaten my security and my sense of identity. My center is within myself; my capacity for being and expressing my essential powers is part of my character structure and depends upon me.[2]

In other words, he is at peace with himself, and his security comes from who he is and not from what he has. But not so with King Saul. First Samuel 18:12, 15, tells us that "Saul was afraid of David, because the LORD was with David . . . When Saul saw how successful he [David] was, he was afraid of him."

MISTRUSTED MOTIVES

Filled with anger at David's success, King Saul thought, *What more can he get but the kingdom?* "And from that time on Saul kept a jealous eye on David" (1 Sam. 18:8–9). An insecure person is always suspicious of the motives and integrity of others. Remember what the devil said when God bragged on Job and his faithfulness? "Does Job fear God for nothing?" (Job 1:9). The Hebrew word translated "nothing" literally means "out of favor." In other words, according to Satan, Job served God only because of the payoff. Satan went on to say, "Have you not put a hedge around him and his household and everything he has? You have blessed the work of his hands, so that his flocks and herds are spread throughout the land. But stretch out your hand and strike everything he has, and he will surely curse you to your face" (vv. 10–11). The devil is suspicious of anyone who serves the Lord. He can't believe that anyone would do it for nothing. No man will be good for nothing. There must be an ulterior motive, a hidden agenda. He's after something. It's easy for the good to be good when they have the goods. "Follow the money and you'll find the motive" is the devil's philosophy. Unfortunately the devil is too often right.

And more unfortunately many have been seduced by his credo. Everyone has a hidden agenda, he tells us. Insecurity and mistrust nestle in the same heart. Insecurity begets mistrust of others, probably because the insecure person operates with ulterior motives—to gain attention or affirmation or position. Many adhere to the attitude "If he's for it, I'm against it," whatever it might be. Some people would vote against the Second Coming if the wrong person proposed it.

The last church I pastored experienced the blessings of God such as I had never seen. God moved in a genuine spiritual awakening that filled the air with the aroma of His presence. One of the most outstanding things God did was to establish what I called "the relationship of a trusted motive." By that I mean we simply trusted each other's motives. Although I made some mistakes in my leadership, the people never doubted my motive for doing what I did.

41

Hence, they were patient and understanding when I goofed. What more could any pastor ask from his people? To me, it was liberating. When I saw two or three deacons in a corner whispering to each other, I didn't become suspicious. Unless there was something special happening, I stopped going to the monthly finance committee meetings. When I mentioned that to a fellow pastor, he gasped in horror. "I would never let them meet without me!" he roared. But I trusted their motives, and they trusted mine. Often the chairman would come to me after a meeting and inform me of an action they were considering. "But," he would say, "we didn't want to do anything without your okay."

The British author Graham Greene said, "It is impossible to go through life without trust: that is to be in the worst cell of all, oneself."

Of course, the gold of this kind of trust must be earned. But people are usually more discerning than we think they are—they will soon enough learn whether or not we are trustworthy.

PERSONAL AMBITION

David wasn't after the throne, yet Saul imagined that he was. "What more can he get but the kingdom?" (1 Sam. 18:8). Saul's world was defined by his selfish ambition; he could not imagine somebody not wanting what he wanted; therefore, he superimposed his diseased thinking upon David. He was determined to keep the kingdom at all costs, even if it meant killing his most loyal subject. That's what selfish and petty ambition does to the soul. One so consumed will risk murder of the life or the reputation by spear or word to gratify his lust. No wonder ambition has been called the last infirmity of noble minds.

I'm not suggesting that ambition is wrong. Not at all. I believe it is a God-given drive, but like all our natural drives, it must be controlled; as is the case in dealing with a hungry circus tiger, we must make sure the lock is secure. Personal, petty, and selfish ambition that is willing to crush others to gain or retain position has no place in the body of Christ.

On the contrary, Paul told us that we should have the attitude of Christ in our interactions with one another. He drove the dagger into the heart of petty ambition when he said, "Do nothing out of selfish ambition or vain conceit, but in humility consider others better than yourselves. Each of you should look not only to your own interests, but also to the interests of others" (Phil. 2:3–4). Some say Christianity has failed, but reading these words, I have to say Christianity hasn't been tried.

TALKING WITHOUT DISCRETION AND LISTENING WITHOUT DISCERNMENT

David and his men were hiding deep within a cave. Suddenly Saul, who was pursuing David, stepped into the cave to relieve himself. Refusing to kill the king as his men urged him, David crept up unnoticed and cut off a corner of Saul's robe. When Saul left the cave, David followed and cried out to the king, "Why do you listen when men say, 'David is bent on harming you'?" (1 Sam. 24:9). To any rational person, that would have been proof enough of David's innocence, but burning with envy, Saul was only too willing to listen to the words of liars. Those men talked without discretion, and Saul listened without discernment.

As a pastor, I instituted a practice that I learned from my childhood pastor. When someone came to my office to accuse another member of moral or spiritual failure, I immediately raised my hand and stopped him. Then I reached for the phone and asked my secretary to get the accused person on the phone. Startled, my visitor would ask what I was doing.

"I'm calling this member you are accusing. I think it's only right for him to be here to hear what you have to say, don't you?"

Without fail my visitor would sputter and stand up, saying it really wasn't that big a deal; he didn't want to get involved. He would flee my office, still muttering excuses.

I would rather pastor a church full of alcoholics than a church full of gossips. Far more damage has been wrought in the church by gossips than by alcoholics or even infidels. Probably no other scriptural admonitions are taken less seriously by believers than those against gossip, slander, and backbiting. During World War II, warning signs were posted in every harbor area: "Loose lips sink ships." There ought to be signs in our churches that warn, "Loose lips sink lives."

Jesus' stern words in Matthew 5 ought to sober us up: "Anyone who says, 'You fool!' will be in danger of the fire of hell" (v. 22). When I was a kid, that verse scared me to death. I thought if I ever slipped and called someone a fool, I would go to hell. And I did that to my best friend. While we were playing, we got into a fist-fight; he was bigger and I lost the fight. Lying on my back, I yelled, "You fool!" And the minute I said that awful word, I thought I was bound for hell. I did a lot of praying after that. But that's not what Jesus means by these words. The word translated "fool" indicates a moral fool; it is to slander or cast doubt upon someone's moral character. Basically Jesus is telling us that casting doubt on a person's moral character is a hell-deserving sin. That can be done with a lie, a half-truth, a suggestion, or a raised eyebrow. With the gossip, every word murders a reputation. God hates a lying tongue; it is an abomination to Him (Prov. 6:16–19).

But we are swift to hear a juicy story about someone else and even swifter to pass it on. Ouida, a nineteenth-century novelist, observed, "A cruel story runs on wheels, and every hand oils the wheels as they run."

Folks have a tendency to see only one side of an issue, and they usually believe the first side they hear. David rarely got to tell his side.

Paul said, "Each of you must put off falsehood and speak truthfully to his neighbor, for we are all members of one body" (Eph. 4:25). Notice the motivation for honesty and truthful speech: "for we are all members of one body." Oh, the foolishness of the gossip who, in wounding others, wounds himself and drinks the same poison he administers to others, then later puzzles why he is in pain.

Plautus, the Roman dramatist, didn't pull any punches when he declared, "Slander-mongers and those who listen to slander, if I had my way, would all be strung up, the talkers by the tongue, the listeners by the ears."

This list isn't exhaustive; there may be many reasons why a friend decides to hurl a spear your way, but I have good news for you. God delivered David from the hand of Saul. David sang his song: "You have delivered me from the attacks of my people; you have preserved me as the head of nations" (2 Sam. 22:44). David could sing such a song because earlier he said, "The LORD has dealt with me according to my righteousness; according to the cleanness of my hands he has rewarded me" (v. 21).

God will deliver you from friendly fire if you react righteously in that situation.

PART 2

SURVIVING
FRIENDLY FIRE

A wounded heart can with difficulty be healed.
—GOETHE

But there is no veil like light and no adamantine armor
against hurt like the truth.
—GEORGE MacDONALD

REPRISE

So you have been wounded by friendly fire. Now you have a choice.

Do you know what roly-poly bugs are? They are the little gray bugs you find in your garage or on your sidewalk. When you get near them, they roll up into little balls. I guess they think you can't see them if they roll up, but all they do is make themselves easier targets to smash! Wounded people often do the same thing—they roll themselves into little balls, turning inward, hiding from the world, thinking that will keep them safe. But in reality, they become even easier targets for anger, bitterness, and self-pity.

Many wounded souls toughen their hides and their hearts, refusing to trust or love anyone ever again. They won't let anyone get close to them, and they certainly are not going to get close to anyone else. There's danger in that behavior. If the wound happened within a church, they may move to another church or stop going altogether. Often wounded ministers leave the ministry. They want to cry with Jeremiah,

Oh, that I had in the desert
a lodging place for travelers,
so that I might leave my people
and go away from them;
for they are all adulterers,
a crowd of unfaithful people.
They make ready their tongue
like a bow, to shoot lies. (JER. 9:2–3)

Better a motel clerk than an unappreciated prophet.

Wounded people who roll up into little balls become distrustful and suspicious, and if they aren't careful, they will end up as spear-throwers.

Their lives become defined by their wounds, continually feeding on the undeserved hurt.

That's one choice. Or you can choose as David did: react righteously, and allow God to deliver and heal you. Victim or victor—it's your choice. Jesus said the truth would set us free, and in the next chapters we will examine scriptural truth that can indeed set you free.

CHAPTER 5

WHEN YOU ARE
TREATED UNFAIRLY

I talked with a man who told me he had left the church where he was a member. When I asked him why, he replied that the church was saturated with power struggles and political strife and that he had been treated unfairly.

"What are you doing now?" I asked.

"Oh, I'm visiting around." An embarrassed smile crossed his face. "I guess I'm looking for the perfect church."

"Yes," I said, "but if you join it, it won't be perfect any longer, will it?" He didn't think that was nearly as funny as I did.

Let's face it: there is no such thing as a perfect church. The church is made up of imperfect human beings with different thoughts, beliefs, and philosophies. In such an atmosphere there are going to be conflicts. In all probability somewhere along the line, we are going to be mistreated. And it has always been this way—even in the New Testament church. In the Galatian church they were, in Paul's words, "biting and devouring each other" (Gal. 5:15). "Biting" and "devouring" suggest wild animals engaged in a deadly struggle. I often hear people lament, "Oh, if we could just get back to the New Testament church." Well, sometimes there's not that great of a difference between that church and ours.

So the real question is not, "Will I be treated unfairly?" but, "What should I do when I am?" Let me offer some suggestions.

DON'T BE SURPRISED

Peter advised his readers, "Dear friends, do not be surprised at the painful trial you are suffering, as though something strange were happening to you." Mistreatment is not something foreign or alien to the Christian life. As a matter of fact, rather than being alien, such trials are native to the Christian character. Remember the Beatitudes (Matt. 5:3–12)? The eighth and final one states, "Blessed are those who are persecuted." In the Beatitudes, Jesus described Christian character. The believer is poor in spirit, mourns, is meek, hungers and thirsts after righteousness, is merciful, is pure in heart, and is a peacemaker. What a wonderful person! And what happens to such a person? He is persecuted.

But trials are also true to our calling. Speaking of trials and sufferings, Peter said, "To this you were called" (1 Peter 2:21). Many people believe the Bible because they don't know what it says. *Called to suffering!* Surely not. But we are called to trials just as truly as we are called to blessings.

The apostle Paul made an interesting statement in Philippians 1:29: "It has been granted [a gift of grace] to you on behalf of Christ not only to believe on him, but also to suffer for him." Suffering for Christ is just as much a part of being saved as is believing. They are gifts of grace.

Through the years, I lost track of a friend from seminary days, so I asked a mutual friend about him. He said, "Oh, he left the ministry several years ago."

"Why?" I asked.

"He had a bad experience in the church."

A bad experience! What did my friend expect? That he would have nothing but wonderful experiences in the ministry? I do not know of a single minister who has not suffered from bad experiences in the ministry. I fantasized what would have happened if Jesus had returned to heaven after a couple of years of ministry. Surprised, the angels might have asked Him, "Lord, why have You returned before Your work was completed?" And Jesus would have said, "Oh, I had a bad experience on earth. I was sorely mistreated."

If it happened to our Lord, it will happen to us. Don't be surprised.

DON'T BE VINDICTIVE

Our natural response to spiritual abuse is to get even (we'll speak more of this later), but that must not be our reaction.

Again Peter instructed us: "It is commendable if a man bears up under the pain of unjust suffering because he is conscious of God. But how is it to your credit if you receive a beating for doing wrong and endure it? But if you suffer for doing good and you endure it, this is commendable before God" (1 Peter 2:19–20). Being right doesn't give us the right to get even. We are to "bear up under the pain" and "endure it." To bear it with patience is the idea. Peter made several points. To bear it with patience is "commendable." The word here is *grace*, and it is used in this context for what is admirable, enhancing the esteem in which those who display it are held. Nothing builds up the reputation of the believer as does enduring mal-treatment with patience.

We do this because we are "conscious of God," Peter said. The New Revised Standard Version reads, "being aware of God." As Christians, we are always to live in the con-sciousness of God's presence; everything we do, we do in the presence of God. And being aware of His presence will make a difference in the way we will act and react. In my younger years, an evangelist visiting our church asked me and the other teenagers, "Would you act differently on your date if your mother were riding in the backseat?" I never did care much for that preacher, but he made a valid point.

When I was a pastor, our church had a great basketball team. One day one of our best players, a tall, lanky fellow we called Bones, came to see me.

"What can I do for you, Bones?" I asked.

"Well, Pastor, I have this problem. It's my mouth, my

language. I can't seem to say a sentence without cussing, and I don't know what to do about it."

I was surprised, for I had never heard him use any bad language. "But, Bones," I said. "I've never heard you curse. I've sat on the bench next to you at games, and many a time there have been situations, bad calls and such, where if a person cursed, he would have done so. I never heard you doing anything like that."

Bones looked appalled. "Of course not! I would never use language like that around you. You're the preacher!"

I said, "Bones, your problem is, you have more respect for me than you do for God, for God is always present, always a witness to everything you do. And if you were as aware of His presence as you are of mine, you would never use foul language."

Peter finished his argument by saying that we should endure wrong patiently because of the example of Christ: "To this you were called, because Christ suffered for you, leaving you an example, that you should follow in his steps" (v. 21). When He was insulted, He didn't retaliate. When He suffered, He didn't threaten His tormentors. Instead He entrusted Himself to the One who judges righteously. As far as Peter was concerned, that should settle the entire issue. And so it should.

DON'T BE INTIMIDATED

"Who is going to harm you if you are eager to do good? But even if you should suffer for what is right, you are blessed.

'Do not fear what they fear; do not be frightened'" (1 Peter 3:13–14). We may not know the Bible, but the Bible sure knows us. It knows exactly how we will react to unfair treatment. So its command is, don't be agitated, irritated, or intimidated. Don't let it shake you up. Why not? Because no one can harm you. "Who is going to harm you if you are eager to do good?"

That's interesting, because in the very next verse Peter declared, "But even if you should suffer for what is right, you are blessed." In one verse he said no one can harm us, and in the next he said we may suffer. I don't know about you, but suffering sounds like harm to me. John said much the same thing speaking of the one born of God: "The evil one cannot harm him" (1 John 5:18).

How do we reconcile this? Even if people cause us to suffer, they cannot harm us because the only real harm is to our character, our love and commitment to God, our inner life. "The body they may kill," proclaims Martin Luther's hymn "A Mighty Fortress Is Our God," but they cannot touch the real you, what you are on the inside. Rather than being harmful, mistreatment is a blessing ("you are blessed," Peter assured) because such treatment forces us to a deeper trust in God. That's why James told us that when we fall into various trials, we are to "consider it pure joy" (James 1:2). How in the world can we do that? Because we know something that others do not know. We know that "the testing of your faith develops perseverance. Perseverance must finish its work so that you may be mature [Greek, perfect] and complete, not lacking anything" (James 1:3–4). Without knowing it, those who cause us to suffer are doing us a favor—they are cooperating with God in making us mature and complete, lacking nothing. The simple truth is, we are better off having suffered than if we had never suffered at all. Did you know the Bible taught such a thing?

DO RESPOND AS CHRIST WOULD

"But in your hearts set apart Christ as Lord. Always be prepared to give an answer to everyone who asks you to give the reason for the hope that you have" (1 Peter 3:15). If our reputation or comfort is not in the Lord, then we will be shaken when we are treated unfairly. We will respond with anger, fear, and vindictiveness. But if Christ is truly Lord, we will react in a Christlike manner, and that reaction will cause people to ask questions concerning our faith and hope. Be prepared to give an answer, Peter urged, for they will surely ask. In short, being mistreated provides one of our greatest opportunities to witness to others.

Sooner or later, you will be mistreated. Be ready by setting apart Christ as Lord in your heart.

CHAPTER 6

MAKE SURE THE WOUND
IS NOT SELF-INFLICTED

I just didn't have the nerve to do it.

I stood there with my legs spread slightly and my feet planted firmly, my left arm hanging loose at my side, my right arm bent with my right hand hovering over the butt of the Colt .44 single-action Peacemaker resting in its holster. I was considering an Old West quick draw.

My hobby is guns—collecting, shooting, and reloading them. I've shot everything from pistols, revolvers, rifles, and shotguns to machine guns. But I had never done a quick-draw shoot. Quick-draw shooting is drawing the gun from the holster (as fast as you can naturally), cocking the hammer as you draw, and then once having cleared the holster, shooting from the hip, just like Marshal Dillon. If you ever saw the TV series *Gunsmoke*, you'll remember the opening shot of Matt Dillon standing in the foreground with his back to the viewer as he faced a bad guy in the dusty street of

Dodge City. Then suddenly they would draw (a quick draw) and shoot. The man with the fastest draw won the battle, which Matt Dillon always did.

Among many gun enthusiasts it is a sport, this quick-draw exercise. I once met the champion of this sport. He could draw his gun, fire, hit the target, and have his gun back in the holster in four-hundredths of a second! That's fast. The only problem is that as you're pulling the gun out of the holster, at the same time cocking the hammer, your thumb can slip from the hammer, causing the gun to fire before you've completed the draw. The result: a .44 lead slug in the foot. When that happens, you can count on losing a couple of toes and walking with a limp the rest of your life. And besides that, it really hurts.

In dry runs with an unloaded gun, my thumb slipped from the hammer most of the time, so I never tried a real quick draw. I didn't want to shoot myself in the foot.

Of course, I have shot myself in the foot—a number of times—but not with a gun.

When I was still pastoring, a member's husband died while I was away at a conference. He had not been a member of the church, so I was not called back to perform the funeral. After I did return, I was so immersed in other things, it didn't occur to me to visit the widow and her daughter, faithful members of our church. A few weeks later, I noticed a distinct coolness in their attitude when I greeted them at church. Obviously something was wrong. Then I realized what it was—my failure to visit the grieving widow and daughter, which is one of the it-goes-without-saying tasks of a minister. I neglected them at a critical moment in their lives. Their offended state was not their fault. I had shot myself in the foot; the wound was self-inflicted. Only after I went to them, apologized, and asked their forgiveness was fellowship restored.

OUR OWN WORST ENEMY

Dr. J. Harold Smith was my pastor as I was growing up. He was (and still is) a bold, passionate preacher with a magnetic personality. But not everyone was drawn to the magnet. A small but powerful group of men opposed him at every turn.

On his fifth anniversary a great celebration was planned. To everyone's surprise (and to some people's horror), Dr. Smith announced in the local newspaper that Sunday night he was going to name the man who had given him the most trouble the past five years. And nobody doubted that he would.

I was in the choir that night and had an unobstructed view of the sanctuary. The place was packed, people sealed in as tightly as a bar of motel soap. A few men had brought their lawyers with them.

Dr. Smith came to the pulpit and announced his text— Romans 7:24: "O wretched man that I am! who shall deliver me from the body of this death?" (KJV). Then while everyone held his breath, Dr. Smith said, "The man in this church who has given me the most trouble for the past five years is . . . J. Harold Smith!"

I saw a sign in a store the other day that read: "If tonight you kick in the seat of the pants the person who caused you the most trouble today, you won't be able to sit down tomorrow."

A pastor told me that his church fired him "because they couldn't take the preaching of the Word." I sympathized with him until I heard him preach. He did preach the Word but with such a negative, self-righteous, condemning attitude that I would have voted for his dismissal. They weren't rejecting the Word; they were rejecting the obnoxious way in which he preached it.

One pastor told me he had just recently realized that the problems he was facing in his church were problems of his own making. That's true of many of us.

But one point should be made clear: offending people will not always be avoidable. In an attempt to reach the unchurched and the younger generation, some churches have created what they call seeker-friendly services. Nothing wrong with that. But some have gone so far as to promise not to say or do anything that would offend. Some have abandoned biblical preaching and have turned to therapeutic preaching, where the sermon is nothing but a Sunday supplement to the newspaper. One pastor told me he never mentions the Cross or sin because it is offensive to unbelievers.

Well, it's supposed to be! You cannot preach the full counsel of God (including man's sin and Christ's cross) without offending some in your congregation. Better to offend man by preaching the gospel than to offend God by watering down the message. When a minister proclaims the gospel in the Spirit and love, if anyone is offended, he need not go to that person and apologize. Rather, he should praise the Lord that the gospel is still the power of God to those who believe. As Paul put it, it is a fragrance: to those who are saved, an aroma of life; to those who are lost, an aroma of death. Death is as viable a response to the gospel as life (2 Cor. 2:15–16).

A CHANGING CULTURE

In our changing culture, as we become surrounded by more and more ethnic groups, we must be more careful about the language we use. Now I'm not advocating political correctness. I hate that philosophy, but nonetheless we must put a guard on our tongues, lest careless speech wound others. Many jokes that were at one time funny are now only offensive to some of our friends and coworkers. You may say, "Well, they ought not to be so thin-skinned." That may be true, but the Bible commands us to "make every effort to live in peace with all men" (Heb. 12:14).

Some of us are so preoccupied with ourselves that we fail to notice the needs and pains of others. The old saying, "To have friends, you must be a friend," is packed with truth. Our thoughtlessness and carelessness, our abrasive ways and rudeness, our failure to acknowledge our friends (acting as if we don't see them), our neglect of thanking others for their help and kindness—all can make people who once thought highly of us hurl a spear our way.

JESUS' ORDER OF WORSHIP

What should you do when you are the offending party? Jesus had a suggestion. I call it Jesus' order of worship. Most churches have an order of worship. It usually begins with an organ prelude, followed by a choir anthem, followed by an invocation, and so forth. But in Matthew 5, Jesus said, "If you are offering your gift at the altar and there remember that your brother has something against you, leave your gift there in front of the altar. *First* go and be reconciled to your brother; then come and offer your gift" (vv. 23–24, emphasis added). "Your brother" comes before "your gift." Before you engage in any act of worship, you must first be reconciled with the one who has something against you. *Reconciled* means "to be restored to his favor." This act of reconciliation is indispensable to worship, for the quality of worship is determined by the quality of the worshiper, and the acceptability of the gift is determined by the acceptability of the giver. You initiate reconciliation, and you should do it immediately: "Settle matters quickly" (v. 25).

What would happen if we followed Jesus' order of worship? The preacher would not preach, the teacher would not teach, the choir would not sing, and the worshipers would not worship until there was reconciliation. The Sunday morning worship might not get under way until late that evening, but what a worship service it would be! By the way, if you're still worrying about whose fault it is, you're not ready. If you're ready for this, then you're ready for the next step.

CHAPTER 7

COMMIT THE SITUATION
TO GOD

The Christian life is largely a matter of reaction. Generally the world doesn't pay a lot of attention to how we act—and given the right circumstances, most of us can act right. But it is our reaction to adverse circumstances that catches the world's attention. When a crisis invades our lives, that's when others pay close attention to how we react. Are we going to react as those in the world would, or does faith really make a difference?

What would you consider the most striking difference between the saved and the lost? Or to put it another way, what would you consider to be the greatest testimony a believer can give to an unbelieving world? I believe it is the way the believer reacts to adversity. Second Samuel 12 records the death of David's baby. When the prophet Nathan told him that because of David's sin, the Lord was going to strike the child with a terminal illness, David immediately fell to the floor and spent seven nights lying there, pleading for the child's life. When the baby finally succumbed to the illness, his servants were afraid to tell him. They said, "While the child was still living, we spoke to David but he would not listen to us. How can we tell him the child is dead? He may do something desperate" (12:18).

But of course, they did tell him. When David heard the dreaded news, he got up, took a shower, splashed on some cologne, changed his clothes, and went to church and worshiped the Lord. Then he went home and ate dinner. Now watch the servants' response: "*Why are you acting this way?* While the child was alive, you fasted and wept, but now that the child is dead, you get up and eat!" (12:21, emphasis added).

ACT OR REACT?

Much of the Sermon on the Mount deals with reactions. For example, "If someone strikes you on the right cheek, turn to him the other also. And if someone wants to sue you and take your tunic, let him have your cloak as well" (Matt. 5:39–40). These were revolutionary words in Jesus' day and remain so today. They definitely do not describe the world's way of responding.

The apostle Peter urged us to follow the example of Jesus, who "when they hurled their insults at him, he did not retaliate; when he suffered, he made no threats. Instead, he entrusted himself to him who judges justly" (1 Peter 2:23).

Again the choice is yours. You may react with shock, shock that someone you loved or trusted would betray you. It may be such a shock that you refuse to believe it happened. Psychologists call this denial.

Or you may react with hurt and humiliation. Perhaps you wept before the person, and in a moment of weakness that only concealed grief can produce, you confided a dark side of yourself or your spouse or your child, and now he has exposed that to others—or maybe not yet and you live in fear that he will, and worse, that others will believe what they are told.

You may react with anger and a desire for vengeance. In my book *When Heaven Is Silent,* I told about being robbed and shot at in a motel parking lot. After the episode, a friend, who fought in Vietnam and was captured by the enemy, called me and told me exactly the emotions I was feeling. He said, "First, there is fear, then humiliation, and then there is rage, the drive to strike back, to get even." He was right on target.

Or you may follow the example of Jesus and entrust yourself to Him who judges justly. That's what David did. In 1 Samuel 24, while Saul was pursuing David, David had an opportunity to kill Saul in a cave, an opportunity that his friends urged him to take. Instead David just cut off a corner of Saul's robe and showed it to him as proof he wasn't after his life or his throne. Listen to David's words: "May the LORD judge between you and me . . . May the LORD be our judge and decide between us" (vv. 12, 15).

I confess David is a better man than I. The man who is trying to kill you is so close, you can touch his robe. If you can cut his robe, you can cut his throat. Justifiable homicide, no doubt about it. But this man after God's own heart chose to let God settle the issue. He refused to take matters into his own hands.

But can God be trusted to handle this violation of trust? Sure, the Bible says that vengeance belongs to God, but what if He doesn't collect the bill? Can we really leave this incident with God? That's exactly what the Scriptures command us to do.

Here is a much-loved and oft-quoted promise: "Commit thy way unto the LORD; trust also in him; and he shall bring it to pass" (Ps. 37:5 KJV). The Hebrew word translated "way" can also be rendered "reputation." I like that. "Commit your reputation to the Lord." And the word translated "commit" means "to roll onto." So we have this injunction: "Roll onto the Lord your reputation." It is the picture of a man shouldering an unbearable burden, and he rolls it off his shoulders onto the Lord. And a reputation is a heavy burden. "A good name is better than fine perfume," declared Solomon (Eccl. 7:1). A lost reputation is almost impossible to recover. Perhaps Rhett Butler was right when he said in *Gone with the Wind*, "Until you've lost your reputation, you never realize what a burden it was or what freedom really is."

The apostle Peter had a word for us: "So then, those who suffer according to God's will should commit themselves to their faithful Creator and continue to do good" (1 Peter 4:19). The word translated "commit" is a commercial term, meaning to "entrust." In biblical days if you were leaving on a long journey, you would deposit your funds and valuables with a trusted friend, and he would secure them while you were away. Is there anything more valuable than your reputation? Entrust your reputation to God who is faithful, and He will protect it. "And continue to do good," Peter said. I've seen many people who have been hurt or mistreated or their reputation called into question, and they simply shut down and no longer attempted to serve God.

REPUTATION—A BURDEN?

Some years ago, our family was getting ready to leave for Sunday evening worship when our eldest son came loping down the stairs wearing a white T-shirt, old blue jeans with portholes in the knees, and tennis shoes in the last stages of leprosy. When my wife saw this apparition, she blurted out: "What are you doing?"

"Going to church," he said.

"Not like *that* you're not!"

"Oh, Mom, all the kids dress like this on Sunday night." (Unfortunately, he was right.)

And then—I'll never forget her words—my wife said, "What kind of mother will people think I am if I let you go to church like that?"

She was expressing what we all feel. "What will people think of me?" The burden of reputation.

In a Colorado conference I talked to a woman whose husband had left her and their son. She was left alone to raise the boy. When he turned sixteen, he rebelled against her, the church, and society, and he was at that time exploring the wonderful world of drugs. She was crying for help. I said, "I'm here only a couple of days. You need someone here who can help you through this. Have you talked to your pastor?"

"Oh, yes," she said.

"What did he say?"

"He said that if I had been a better mother, my son wouldn't be doing these things."

That was certainly encouraging to her, I'm sure! The ironic thing is that when the pastor's son reached sixteen, he did the same thing. Now when that happens, it can do one of two things to you: it can humble you, which is good, or it can humiliate you, which is bad. In the pastor's case, he was humiliated to the extent that he resigned his pastorate. Having been acquainted with this man for a number of years, I knew he was grieved over his son's condition. But what grieved him most was the harm he felt had been done to his reputation. In other words, he was more concerned with his reputation than with his son's rebellion. Often what concerns us most is not the bad thing that happens, but the *effect* that thing will have on our reputations.

Well, you don't want to lose your reputation, which is probably what will happen if you take matters into your own hands. But what is the alternative? Roll it onto the Lord. Commit to God your reputation. And guess what? He says if you will do this, He will "make your righteousness shine like

70

the dawn, the justice of your cause like the noonday sun [the brightest hour of the day]" (Ps. 37:6). That is a promise of vindication. You try to vindicate yourself, and you'll mess it up every time. God will vindicate you if your cause is just.

Wasn't that what Paul did? In response to friendly fire from some of the brethren at Corinth, he said, "I care very little if I am judged by you or by any human court; indeed, I do not even judge myself. My conscience is clear, but that does not make me innocent. It is the Lord who judges me" (1 Cor. 4:3–4). What a burden-lifting thing it is to be able to say, "I care little if I am judged by you." What liberation from a load!

Where did Paul learn how to react? From Christ. In reading the passages describing His mock trial before His accusers, I am struck by how Jesus kept silent, refusing to defend Himself. Luke recorded Jesus' appearance before Herod: "When Herod saw Jesus, he was greatly pleased, because for a long time he had been wanting to see him. From what he had heard about him, he hoped to see him perform some miracle. He plied him with many questions, but Jesus gave him no answer" (Luke 23:8–9).

I remember as a kid sitting in the balcony of the Temple Theater in my hometown, seeing for the first time the old black-and-white silent movie *The King of Kings,* presented by Cecil B. DeMille. I knew the story, knew how it turned out, but I couldn't bear for Jesus to do nothing. When Herod asked Him to perform a miracle, I found myself saying, "Do it, Jesus, do it! They will know who You are and You'll get out of this mess. Dazzle old Herod with a miracle and You'll go free!" But Jesus gave no answer. Self-defense was not a part of His program.

STAND STILL AND GO FORWARD

In one church I pastored years ago, there existed a group of people who didn't like me. Unbelievable, isn't it? But there are strange people in every church. After a while, members of this group began to say really not-so-nice things about me, trying to draw others to their side. One of my staff members said I should confront them.

And I would have done so if I hadn't just finished studying Exodus 14. Having led the people out of Egypt, Moses brought them to the Red Sea. In the meantime Pharaoh had a change of heart. "What have we done?" he said. "We have let the Israelites go and have lost their services!" (v. 5). He mounted a mighty army to recapture them (you can always count on the devil to try to recapture lost ground). When the Israelites saw the Egyptians, they immediately blamed Moses: "Well, Pastor, here's another fine mess you've gotten us into. Not enough room to bury us in Egypt? So you brought us out here?"

But Moses had a word from the Lord: stand still and move forward. "Do not be afraid," Moses said. "Stand firm and you will see the deliverance the LORD will bring you today. The Egyptians you see today you will never see again. The LORD will fight for you; you need only to be still" (vv.

13–14). Then God commanded Moses to go forward and cross the sea.

Basically God was saying, "Moses, I didn't save you from Egypt to fight Egyptians. I saved you to go forward and possess the land. Don't worry about the Egyptians; I will take care of them." One of the most effective strategies of the devil is to get us spending all our time and energy fighting the Egyptians who are nipping at our heels, therefore leaving neither time nor energy to do what God saved us to do: go forward.

I didn't confront my Egyptians. I committed them to the Lord and focused my efforts on going forward. Faithful to His word, the Lord raised up a shield against the spears of my "friendly enemies."

Not long ago I saw a movie about World War II. There was one scene where the Americans and Germans were fighting close together. It was humorous to me because the Germans would throw grenades at the Americans, the Americans would throw them back at the Germans, and vice versa. Each side kept throwing the enemy's grenades back at the other. Now that's a wise thing to do in military combat.

But we like to do the same thing in spiritual combat. If someone throws a grenade at us, we immediately throw it back, hoping it will blow him away. Instead of throwing back to the enemy the grenades he has thrown, let's pitch them to God and let Him handle them. This is what it means to commit the act to God. If we trust Him with the grenades, He will fight for us.

CHAPTER 8

UNMASK YOUR IDOLS

It is the most subtle of all sins.

It is the sin beneath all other sins.

It wears many disguises.

It is idolatry.

Tertullian, who was an early church father, said, "The principal crime of the human race, the highest guilt charged upon the world, the whole procuring cause of judgment, is idolatry."

To survive friendly fire, we must unmask our idols.

I know what you must be saying: "Hey, there are no sacred cows in my home, no pagan altars, no graven images to which I bow down and worship." And you're right. "Besides," you say, "idolatry has nothing to do with my surviving the wounds I have received." There, I believe, you may be wrong.

It is significant that the last words of 1 John, a letter written to believers, are, "Dear children, keep yourselves from idols" (5:21). And to the Corinthians, Paul wrote, "Therefore, my dear friends, flee from idolatry" (1 Cor. 10:14). Do you remember the challenge of Joshua to the people? "Throw away the gods your forefathers worshiped beyond the River and in Egypt" (Josh. 24:14). What is so interesting about this is that none of the people he was addressing had ever been in Egypt! Yet they were still worshiping Egyptian gods. Subtle and pervasive are these gods. In truth, we are never far from worshiping idols. Richard Keyes calls the heart an idol factory: "Like someone held at gunpoint with his own pistol, Christians have been threatened and attacked for two hundred years on the basis of their own view of idolatry, turned against them."[1]

WHAT IS AN IDOL?

When we think of idols, our minds conjure up pictures of animals or humans or graven images made of stone or wood. But idols occupy not only pagan altars but also the heart and mind. Idolatry is a master of disguise. If we fail to understand its true nature, we will be unable to recognize it in our lives, and it will be free to corrupt and distort every aspect of our Christian life.

So we need a definition of an idol. Richard Keyes offers this: "An idol is something within creation that is inflated to function as a substitute for God. All sorts of things are potential idols . . . An idol can be a physical object, a property, a person, an activity, a role, an institution, a hope, an image, an idea, a pleasure, a hero."[2]

Stephen Charnock put it on an even more personal level. Each person "acts as if God could not make him happy without the addition of something else. Thus the glutton makes a god of his dainties; the ambitious man of his honor; the incontinent man of his lust; the covetous man of his wealth; and consequently esteems them as his chiefest good, and the most noble end to which he directs his thoughts . . . All men worship some golden calf, set up by education, custom, natural inclination and the like."[3]

"God could not make him happy without the addition of something else." Do you need something besides God to make you happy? Is it Jesus plus something else? While we may not verbalize it, we may be saying, "Lord, I'm grateful that I have You, but You Yourself are not enough. If I am to have peace and joy, I must have this other thing also." That is idolatry. When Christ alone is not sufficient for your joy, you have an idol in your heart. When an undeserved hurt eclipses your joy in Christ, look for an idol.

Again, Keyes says, "Idolatry may not involve explicit denials of God's existence or character. It may well come in the form of an overattachment to something that is, in itself, perfectly good."[4] Modern Christians are much too naive about idolatry. Hardly any of us would admit we are guilty. But idolatry hides itself well.

It is a legitimate desire to be well liked and well thought of. It is a legitimate desire to want friends you can trust. It is a legitimate desire to have a good reputation. And being wounded by friendly fire threatens all of that; it may even take it all away. Suddenly someone has pulled the plug on your joy and carried into captivity your peace. The question is, How much can you subtract from your life and still retain your joy in the Lord? That's when you discover that you have made an idol of your image or your reputation or your honor.

Becoming anxious about undeserved hurts is only natural. But you must understand that such anxiety takes His work out of His hands and focuses your thoughts on your hurts. Aristotle said, "Memory is the scribe of the soul." You remember your injuries, pouring mud into a silver chalice.

Through the years, a great many people have said good things about my ministry and have done good things for me, and to tell the truth, I don't remember all of those people. But I have never forgotten a single person who did me wrong. If you want to make a lasting impression on me, just come up after a service and say, "That was a terrible sermon." I promise I will never forget you. I still remember the man who said to me after one message, "You missed the whole point." My memory immediately erected a monument of dishonor to that fellow.

Anxiety is a shadow cast by an idol, something so important to us that God alone cannot satisfy our hearts. Not only is it an affront to God, but it is the most futile of activities. Someone has said, "We may sooner by our care [anxiousness] add a furlong to our grief, than a foot to our comfort."

DISMANTLING OUR IDOLS AND DISENGAGING OUR ANXIETY

Contentment in Christ is the solution to both our idolatry and our anxiety. And everyone is searching for it. Neil Clark Warren calls it the Grand Search:

> The search I'm talking about is for *enduring* contentment, the kind of deep-down, soul-satisfying contentment that infuses your life with peace and serenity, gives you freedom and energy to express yourself and follow your dreams despite what others may think, and allows you to fall asleep at night without fretting about what might have been.[5]

Divine contentment is a temper of the spirit that enables a believer to keep his poise and composure in any and every circumstance.

THE SECRET OF CONTENTMENT

I am reluctant to use the word *secret* because it is so overused. Everybody is looking for secrets. The word has a magnetic lure. You know those newspaper-magazines at the grocery checkout counter? They are always promising to reveal secrets. "The Beauty Secrets of the Stars." "The Secret Diet of Doctors." You understand that I would never buy one of those things — but I do read mighty fast while I'm in the checkout lane.

But there *is* a secret of contentment. Paul learned it.

While in prison, falsely accused and betrayed by colleagues, he wrote to the Philippians: "I am not saying this because I am in need, for I have learned to be content whatever the circumstances . . . I have learned the *secret* of being content in any and every situation" (Phil. 4:11–12, emphasis added). No wonder he could say to them earlier, "Do not be anxious about anything" (4:6).

The word Paul used for "content" literally means "self-contained." It is to be independent of external circumstances, to have an inner self-sufficiency, requiring no outside assistance. In the ancient world it was used of cities that were self-contained, having their own food and water supplies. In those times when an army laid siege to a city, they would surround it, cutting off supply routes, hoping to starve the people into surrender. But if it was a "contented" city, self-contained, needing no outside resources, it was invulnerable to the siege. Imagine what this would mean to Christians to be independent of outward circumstances, needing no outside resources to be happy. Let the world, the flesh, and the devil do what they may, we would be self-contained. We would no longer be vulnerable to the bribes of the world to compromise our Christian integrity.

The world may say, "If you don't give and take and loosen up on your convictions, we're going to withhold happiness, esteem, promotion, and wealth from you."

"Take your best shot," the Christian says. "I am self-contained. Within me is all I need for fulfillment."

Contentment comes from within, not from foreign comforts. Outward troubles cannot shake the contented heart. To those who have learned this secret, when there is madness without, there is music within. Have you ever been stung by a bee? I'm sure you have. When I was a little boy, an older friend told me that if I caught a bee in my hand, quickly closing my fist on it, it couldn't sting me. We live and learn. But a bee can sting only the skin, the outer layer of the body; it cannot sting the heart. When you are content, friends may sting you with betrayal, but they cannot sting your heart.

I don't think I'm overstating it when I say that divine contentment is a remedy against all our troubles, a support in all our burdens, and a cure for all our anxieties. There is a secret of contentment, but . . .

IT IS A SECRET THAT MUST BE LEARNED

I was afraid of that. I was hoping that I could just pray for contentment, and God would take a magic wand and zap me full of contentment. "I have *learned*," Paul said. And again in Philippians 4:12, he said, "I have *learned* the secret of being content." "I have learned," not "I have heard that I ought to be" or "I believe that I should be." I'm afraid that we Christians hear much but learn little. A person may know much about Christ, but not have learned Him. Sometimes we're just too lazy to learn. Oh, we want to hear, but learning, well, that requires more thought and study than we're willing to give. I remember one church I visited, and I remarked to the pastor, "Your people are great listeners."

"Yes," he said. "They love to hear the Word preached. Of course, they have no intention of doing anything about what they hear. They just love to hear preaching, just as some people love to dance or play golf."

Listening without learning—that's the curse of too much of the church. In Ephesians, Paul spoke about learning Christ (4:20 NKJV). James warned us against listening without learning: "Do not merely listen to the word, and so deceive yourselves. Do what it says" (James 1:22).

Paul used a different word for "learn" in Philippians 4:12 from the one in verse 11. It was a technical word used by the mystery religions of that day. It means "to be instructed or initiated into a mystery." The word indicates a long and difficult process. The tense used by Paul denotes a continuous state. Alexander Souter translates it, "I habituate," indicating a habit of life.[6] Contentment is a habitual thing, a state of being.

What school did Paul attend to learn this lesson? What was the curriculum? He tells us in verse 12: "I know what it is to be in need, and I know what it is to have plenty . . . in any and every situation, whether well fed or hungry, whether living in plenty or in want." Paul made a great discovery: he learned that having everything didn't add anything to him and having nothing didn't take anything from him. He was neither enhanced by riches nor diminished by poverty. This philosophy is so contrary to the world's that we, being in the world, have a difficult time doing anything but paying lip service to it.

The world's idea of finding contentment is by increasing our possessions; God's way is by decreasing our desires. I'm sure that you, like I, have found that the more a person has, the less satisfied he is. True contentment gives a person victory over himself and his desires. The writer of Proverbs told us that he who "ruleth his spirit" is a mightier warrior than "he that taketh a city" (Prov. 16:32 KJV). Such a person is a true hero, a Medal of Honor winner.

THE SECRET OF CONTENTMENT IS CHRIST

There is a secret of contentment, and that secret must be learned. So what is the secret? Christ. "I can do all things through Christ which strengtheneth me" (Phil. 4:13 KJV). I like the Phillips translation here: "I am ready for anything through the strength of the One who lives within me." And Williams's translation reads, "I have power for all things through him who puts a dynamo in me." The word translated "strengtheneth" means "to infuse strength into someone."

Contentment is a divine thing. It comes not by acquisition, but by infusion. Nor does it come through willpower or therapeutic psychology. It comes through Christ. The contented believer is "ready for anything" because the Christ who lives within him is constantly infusing him with supernatural strength. The secret of contentment is Christ. Christ Himself. Christ alone. As always, Christ is the answer.

The great British preacher George Duncan, now in heaven, told me the story of a wealthy Englishman who lost his only son in World War II. A pilot in the RAF, he was shot down during the Battle of Britain. Some years later the elderly man died. Having lost his wife and his only child, he had no heirs, so in his will he directed that his estate be auctioned off and the proceeds given to various charities.

A part of the man's estate was a priceless art collection, and a London auction house arranged for the sale. On the day of the auction, collectors and the curious gathered from many countries, hoping to obtain pieces of the fabulous collection. At the beginning, the portrait of a young man was placed on the easel. The auctioneer explained that the man's will stipulated that before any of the other pieces of art could be sold, the picture—a portrait of the man's son—must be sold first. The crowd was disappointed because the artist was unknown, as was his subject. A valueless work.

The crowd was quiet; no one wanted the portrait. But there happened to be among the curious one of the man's lifelong servants who had known the son from his birth. He thought that it would be nice to have the picture, and since no one else was interested, he could probably get it cheap. So he offered a bid. No one opposed him. The picture was his.

At that moment the auctioneer said, "Ladies and gentlemen, the auction is ended." The people gathered were stunned with disbelief.

The auctioneer explained, "The will further stipulated that whoever got the picture of the son got the whole lot."

Whoever has the Son has the whole lot.

CHAPTER 9

LOOK FOR THE UNSEEN
HAND OF GOD

What I do thou knowest not now; but thou shalt know hereafter.

—JOHN 13:7 KJV

One of my memories as a child is that of my mom sitting for hours on the sofa, crocheting pillowcases (it was before all the timesaving devices were invented, so she still had time to do handiwork). One day I wandered into the living room while my mom was in the kitchen and saw lying on the arm of the sofa one of the pillowcases she was working on. I picked it up and was greeted by a jarring mass of tangled colored threads and knots shooting in all directions, forming no intelligent pattern. It looked like something a madman had done, as though someone had indiscriminately thrust a needle and thread through the material without plan or purpose. Then I flipped the pillowcase over and on the top side was a beautiful picture of a bluebird perched on a leafy tree, singing. I had been looking at the wrong side, which didn't make any sense, but when I looked at the top side, I saw the lovely picture that my mom was weaving.

Has your life ever looked like the bottom side of that pillowcase? Mine has. Just a tangled mass of threads and knots, going everywhere and nowhere, making no sense at all. We've all worn our fingernails down to the quick, trying to discern some reasonable purpose to what is happening in our lives. But our problem is limited view; we're not tall enough to look at the top side. If we could see it from God's angle, we would see that He never wastes time and experience and that every seemingly senseless thread and knot is part of the weaving of God's will for our lives.

John Flavel wrote, "O how ravishing and delectable a sight it will be to behold at one view the whole design of Providence, and the proper place and use of every single act, which we could not understand in this world!"[1]

Providence. Not a word we hear or use much today, almost extinct in today's Christian vocabulary, but one of the richest truths of the Bible concerning God's care for us. Abraham expressed it first when God delivered Isaac from the altar of sacrifice and in his place provided a ram: "And Abraham called the name of that place Jehovah-jireh" (Gen. 22:14 KJV). *Jehovah-jireh* means "the Lord will provide."

WHAT IS PROVIDENCE?

The word comes from a Latin prefix and root. The prefix *pro* means "before" or "in front of." The root *videre* means "to see." Put together, the word means "to see beforehand." But the word indicates more than God's foreknowledge, "to see before"; it indicates "to see before and make provision."

Louis Berkhof defines *providence* as "that continued exercise of the divine energy whereby the Creator preserves all His creatures, is operative in all that comes to pass in the world, and directs all things to their appointed end."[2] Belief in providence is the conviction that the world, rather than being ruled by chance (the Epicurean view) or by fate (the Stoic view), is ruled by a hands-on God, who preserves, protects, provides, and governs His creation so that it accomplishes His preordained purpose. "He governs by his presence what he created by his power."[3] *Providence performs in time what God purposed in eternity.*

We all exercise providence to some extent. That's why we buy life insurance. We know beforehand that we are going to die, and knowing it, we make provision for that need. I have a quirky stomach, and nearly anything I eat gives me heartburn, so an hour before I eat, I take a little pill the doctor prescribed to prevent it from happening. I know beforehand what is going to happen, so I make provision. Speaking of providence, R. C. Sproul says, "It is not merely that God looks at human affairs. The point is that

He looks *after* human affairs. He not only watches us, He watches *over* us."[4]

The Westminster Confession defines the providence of God like this: "God the great Creator of all things doth uphold, direct, dispose, and govern all creatures, actions, and things, from the greatest even to the least, by his most wise and holy providence, according to his infallible foreknowledge, and the free and immutable counsel of his own will, to the praise of the glory of his wisdom, power, justice, goodness, and mercy."[5]

Providence means that God sees beforehand what is going to happen to us, what need is going to arise in our lives, and He makes provision accordingly so that when we arrive at that point of need, the provision will be waiting for us. Think of it! Long before the need appears in your life, God has already made provision.

Think of Creation. God made water before He made fish. He didn't make fish first, then tell them to flop around on the ground while He made water. The water was first, then the fish, the provision before the problem. He made plants and grass before He made creatures that would need them to eat. He made air before He made creatures that would need to breathe. He didn't make animals, then tell them to hold their breath while He came up with air. There was a Garden of Eden before there were a man and a woman. There was Adam's rib before Eve was needed. And there was a cross on Calvary before there was a tree in the midst of the Garden. There was provision for sin before there was sin, for Christ was "slain from the foundation of the world" (Rev. 13:8 NKJV).

> Though troubles assail,
> And dangers affright,
> Though friends should all fail,
> And foes all unite;
> Yet one thing secures us,
> Whatever betide,
> The Scripture assures us,
> The Lord will provide.
>
> (JOHN NEWTON)

THE INVISIBLE HAND

Providence has been called "the invisible hand of God," and because His hand of providence is invisible, we, too, often fail to recognize His active presence in our lives. But God's invisibility does not mean His absence or inactivity.

David learned that truth from his attempts to escape the spear-throwing hand of Saul. David declared, "I will cry unto God most high; unto God that performeth all things for me" (Ps. 57:2 KJV), spoken while he was hiding in a cave, fleeing Saul. One of the Puritan divines translated it: "I will cry unto God most high, unto God, *the transactor of my affairs.*"[6] I like that.

David composed this psalm as he hid in a cave in the wilderness of En Gedi, an obscure and desolate hole, among broken rocks and wild goats. Saul had actually entered the cave where David was hiding. That event probably prompted David to write: "My soul is among lions: and I lie even

89

among them that are set on fire, even the sons of men, whose teeth are spears and arrows, and their tongue a sharp sword" (v. 4 KJV).

He seemed unusually calm in the situation, didn't he? I'll tell you how calm and assured David was. The text tells us that Saul entered the cave to relieve himself. David and his men were back deep in the cave, and his men urged David to sneak up on Saul and slay him. But as we have already seen, David refused to kill the Lord's anointed. David only cut off a corner of Saul's robe and followed Saul out of the cave, holding up the piece of cut cloth and challenging him to let God settle the matter (1 Sam. 24:8–15).

Where did his calm assurance come from? From the unseen hand of God. In the preceding chapter Saul had David trapped. There was no way the sweet singer of Israel could escape. But just as Saul was about to attack, a messenger arrived with news: "Come quickly! The Philistines are raiding the land." Saul had to break off his pursuit of David and do battle with the Philistines (1 Sam. 23:27–28). At the moment of extreme danger, God moved on the Philistines to raid the land, giving Saul no choice but to let David go. That's providence.

WHY IS IT SO DIFFICULT TO SEE THE HIDDEN HAND OF GOD?

I'm convinced some people could stand in the middle of a lake and not see water. And some of us are so focused and insensitive, we could stand in the middle of heaven and not see God! It is possible for Jesus to be present, for us to look straight at Him, yet not see Him. As a matter of fact, the very first person to see the resurrected Lord did not recognize Him.

That person's name was Mary Magdalene, the last one at the cross and the first one at the tomb. The story is told in John 20. On the first day of the week, she came early to the tomb and discovered that the stone had been rolled away. After Peter and John arrived on the scene, they looked into the tomb and saw that the body had been removed. As though there was nothing there for them, they returned home.

"But Mary stood weeping outside the tomb. As she wept, she bent over to look into the tomb; and she saw two angels in white, sitting where the body of Jesus had been lying, one at the head and the other at the feet. They said to her, 'Woman, why are you weeping?' She said to them, 'They have taken away my Lord, and I do not know where they have laid him'" (John 20:11–13 NRSV).

And when she had said that, she turned around and saw Jesus standing there, but didn't know it was Jesus. Jesus asked why she was weeping and whom she sought. "Supposing him to be the gardener, she said to him, 'Sir, if you have carried him away, tell me where you have laid him, and I will take him away.' Jesus said to her, 'Mary!' She turned and said to him in Hebrew, 'Rabbouni!' (which means Teacher)" (John 20:15–16 NRSV). She immediately grabbed hold of Him, not wanting to let go.

Why did she not recognize Him the first time? One

reason that has been suggested was that she could not see Him through her tears. She was "weeping," indicating she was in deep mourning.

It is hard for us to see Jesus through tear-filled eyes. Our vision is blurred and our hearts are preoccupied with grief. Often in times of deep distress, we cannot see straight or think rationally. All we can see is the cause of our distress and wonder where Jesus is. I can't recount the times when people whose eyes were brimming with tears have asked, "Where is God?"

Perhaps we are turned in the wrong direction. Twice, the Scripture says that Mary had to turn to see the Lord. A number of years ago there was a popular song, "Looking for Love in All the Wrong Places." This is a generation that feels emptiness perhaps more than love. Having abundant material possessions, we are learning, does not fill what Augustine called the God-shaped void in man. It's not that we fail to seek. We seek the wrong things and in the wrong places—pleasure, power, money, sex, houses, and cars. Some try to fill that void by drink and drugs.

Another reason it is so difficult to see Him is that we are unable to see God's hand beyond the mere fact of the event. When Mary looked into the tomb, she saw two angels—and was unimpressed. Now if I looked in my closet and saw two angels sitting there, I might get the idea that something divine was going on! Wouldn't you? I mean, if there are angels around, God must be close by. And yet Mary could not see beyond the mere fact that the body was gone. She failed to look beyond the event itself to see that there was more to it than she was seeing.

YOU DO NOT KNOW NOW WHAT I AM DOING

In the Upper Room when Jesus began washing the disciples' feet, Peter was outraged. It was the work of the lowest slave. He vehemently protested, "Lord, you shall not wash my feet!" But Jesus said, "You do not know now what I am doing [Jesus is constantly saying that to us, and it is true], but later you will understand" (John 13:7 NRSV). All Peter could see was the current event—Jesus was washing his feet. So spiritually dull was Peter, he could not imagine that there might be a greater, more significant thing going on than merely the washing of his feet. He could not see beyond the shocking fact that Jesus might be up to something more than washing feet. And He was: He was giving the disciples a lesson in humility, love, and service.

In the Christian life there is always more than meets the eye. Great events lie beyond commonplace incidents.

Of course, Mary's real problem was that she was looking for a corpse rather than a living Lord. She was weeping not over the death of Jesus, but over His disappearance. Jesus was dead; that was an indisputable fact. And if she had found the dead body of Jesus, she would have been satisfied. I'm glad she didn't find what she was looking for!

It's often impossible for us to see the hidden hand of God

because deep down in our hearts we aren't expecting a living Lord to be on the scene, working out all things for our good.

GOD OFTEN EMPLOYS HIS (AND OUR) ENEMIES TO DELIVER US

Things don't always turn out the way you expect. A number of years ago my family and I were planning a vacation. We had a place in mind, but a close friend told us about another place. He described it in such beautiful terms, we decided to go there instead. That's when I learned that beauty is in the eye of the beholder. When we saw it, our spirits died; it was awful, not what we were expecting at all. We spent a miserable week there.

And God does not always work things out the way we expect. Sometimes outward circumstances contradict everything God has said to us; suddenly everything we believe looks like a sham. During the Babylonian captivity, Judah clung to the promise that God would deliver them. And deliver them God did; but not in the way they expected— and not in a way they approved of.

Isaiah 45 tells the story. When the time came for God to deliver His people from Babylon, He chose a pagan king, Cyrus, to do the job. The prophet made it clear that Cyrus was an unbeliever:

> For the sake of Jacob my servant,
>   of Israel my chosen,

I summon you by name
and bestow on you a title of honor,
though you do not acknowledge me. (v. 4, emphasis added)

And again in verse 5, God said, "I will strengthen you, *though you have not acknowledged me*" (emphasis added).

But the people would have none of it. In verse 9, Isaiah spoke of their reaction to the news:

Woe to him who quarrels with his Maker,
to him who is but a potsherd among the potsherds
on the ground.
Does the clay say to the potter,
"What are you making?"
Does your work say,
"He has no hands"?

The word translated "quarrels" means "stubborn opposition, to find fault." It signifies an "I know better" attitude. When they say, "He has no hands," they are really saying, "He's all thumbs." They are accusing Him of incompetence, which is what we always do when we complain about our circumstances. God's toughest task was not to get pagan Cyrus to deliver the people; it was to get His people to accept it. Their pride was offended by being delivered by a pagan king. They would rather have remained in bondage than be delivered God's way.

Interesting, isn't it? We plead with God to rescue us from some evil, and when He doesn't do it the way we want or expect, we rebel. The sad truth is that many of us would rather remain in bondage than be delivered God's way. I know lost people who would rather go to hell than be saved God's way.

Now when God works in unexpected or unacceptable ways, we are in danger of doing two things:

1. We may quarrel or strive with our Maker. We may never actually say the words, but we are, in effect, accusing God of mismanagement. Toward this attitude, God has but one word to say—*woe*.

2. We may simply assume that God is not working. He has turned a deaf ear to our cry, and we are left alone. As I said in an earlier book, people often say to me, "God has finally started working in my life." But that's not true; God is always working in our lives: "Being confident of this, that he who began a good work in you will carry it on to completion until the day of Christ Jesus" (Phil. 1:6). What we mean is, God has finally started acting the way we want Him to act.

So you are in bondage because someone has wronged you, but you have prayed to God that He will deliver you. And He will; you know He will. As a matter of fact, you can see exactly how He is going to do it. But wait—this isn't what you had in mind! He doesn't seem to be working at all, and if He is, you don't like it. What's the solution?

Isaiah told us of God's words: "You shall commit to Me the work of My hands" (45:11 NASB). Like clay on the potter's wheel, we do not advise and consent; we simply trust His wisdom and let Him handle it His own way. But no one can trust like that in a vacuum. There must be a solid basis on which to lay our faith. And the wonderful thing about God is that He never tells us to trust Him without laying before us a firm foundation for that faith. We can't truly trust a person we do not know, and the foundation for our trusting God is knowing what kind of God we are trusting.

We learn more about the Lord from Isaiah:

1. *He is the Lord who does all things*. God said,

> I form the light and create darkness,
> I bring prosperity and create disaster;
> I, *the* LORD, *do all these things*. (Isa. 45:7,
> emphasis added)

Many deny God's total sovereignty to keep Him from being blamed for "unjust" things, but God doesn't seem to worry about what we puny creatures think. He blatantly declared, "I, the LORD, do all these things." God isn't embarrassed by His sovereignty.

He is a sovereign God. He is alone in His sovereignty; He and the devil do not comanage the affairs of history. Even Satan cannot act without God's permission. The first two chapters of Job show us that. A recurring phrase in Isaiah 45 is, "I am the LORD, and there is no other" (vv. 5, 6, 14, 18, 21, 22). I get the idea that God is trying to tell us something—and that something is, "I am the Lord, and there is no other."

He is absolute in His sovereignty. Nothing lies outside His jurisdiction: "God's providence is over all creatures; over fixed and planetary stars; over angels and devils; over saints and sinners; over beasts, and birds, and fishes; over globes and atoms; over heat and cold; over war, famine and pestilence; over heaven, earth, and hell."[7]

2. *He is the Lord who has the right to do all things.* God is not a bully, taking advantage of His size. He is the Creator; we are the creatures. He is the Potter; we are the clay. As Paul said in Romans 9:21, referring to Isaiah 45, "Hath not the potter power over the clay?" (KJV).

God has the right to do what He does. This may be our biggest hurdle in totally committing to Him the work of His hands. When I heard that our eldest son was dead, the first words that popped into my mind—and are inscribed on his headstone—were these: "But our God is in the heavens: he hath done whatsoever he hath pleased" (Ps. 115:3 KJV). Without this acceptance of God's right to do what He pleases, our anger and bitterness will be like a sharpened knife plunged into the heart of faith.

3. *He is the Lord who does all things right.* God said,

> I will raise up Cyrus in my righteousness:
>> I will make all his ways straight.
> He will rebuild my city
>> and set my exiles free,
> but not for a price or reward,
>> says the LORD Almighty. (Isa. 45:13)

God did fulfill His promise; He did keep His word. He did deliver His people. It was all done through Cyrus and it was free! Not only did He bring good to His people, but He brought glory to Himself.

The one grand truth God is seeking to show mankind is this: "I am God, and there is none else." And He did it by making His enemies into His servants. If we will be patient and commit to Him the work of His hands, He will turn our enemies, even "friendly enemies," into our servants. Paul's thorn in the flesh was an enemy to Paul. But rather than remove the thorn, God used it to serve up dishes of grace Paul had never tasted. The poet William Cowper in "Good Moves in Mysterious Ways," wrote:

> Judge not the Lord by feeble sense,
> But trust Him for His grace;
> Behind a frowning providence,
> He hides a smiling face.
>
> His purposes will ripen fast,
> Unfolding every hour;
> The bud may have a bitter taste,
> But sweet will be the flower.
>
> Blind unbelief is sure to err,
> And scan His work in vain;
> God is His own interpreter,
> And He will make it plain.

CHAPTER 10

KEEP HUMMING THE RIGHT TUNE

Two things can pierce the umbrella of the wounded believer's peace: fretting over past hurts and fearing future ones. The present crucified between the past and the future.

But there is a way to plug the holes in the umbrella of peace: meditating on God's providence. To many moderns, meditation is either a lost art or a suspicious practice associated with Eastern religions or the pseudospiritual New Age movement, which is not new at all. But the Bible has much to say about meditating on the things of God. We are told that the person who "meditates" on the law of the Lord will be blessed (Ps. 1:2). The Hebrew word translated "meditate" means to "ponder," "muse," or "hum."

Hum. I like that. It reminds me of an interview of a popular singer I heard several years ago. In the course of the interview, the singer said that it was his practice to constantly hum some tune. "Humming," he said, "keeps the vocal cords limbered up and in tune, so that I can sing at the drop of a hat. Humming is a constant 'warming up' exercise." He continued, "You never know when you're going to be called on to hoist a tune."

In the same way, humming, meditating, constantly pondering the providence of God, will keep us ready to sing praises to His name, no matter how suddenly a problem arises. Whatever it is and whenever it occurs, we are already warmed up.

Meditating upon God's providence, humming the right tune, will give us the serenity of divine design. David hummed himself to sleep at night with this tune: "I remember thee upon my bed, and meditate on thee in the night watches" (Ps. 63:6 KJV). And in Psalm 77:12, "I will meditate on all your works and consider all your mighty deeds." One more time: "I remember the days of long ago; I meditate on all your works and consider what your hands have done" (Ps. 143:5). The apostle Paul exhorted us to do the same thing: "Finally, brothers, whatever is true, whatever is noble, whatever is right, whatever is pure, whatever is lovely, whatever is admirable—if anything is excellent or praiseworthy—think about such things" (Phil. 4:8). Think about—consider, reckon, take into account—these things. The word *think* indicates a continual or habitual activity.

It is true that whatsoever a man thinketh, that he is (Prov. 23:7 KJV). You tell me what you think about all the time, and I'll tell you what kind of person you are. Paul spoke of taking into captivity "every thought to make it obedient to Christ"

(2 Cor. 10:5). And the ancient prophet advised, "Thou wilt keep him in perfect peace, whose mind is stayed on thee: because he trusteth in thee" (Isa. 26:3 KJV).

In my years as a traveling minister, I have stayed in more than a thousand motels. As far as I can remember, every door had a peephole in it so I could see who was knocking on the door. Why? Because we are cautious about the people we let into our rooms. We are also prudent about checking on a visitor before opening the door at home. To open the door to just anyone could prove disastrous, even deadly. It's too bad that we are not that cautious about the thoughts we let into our minds. We open the door to the mind without ever checking the peephole, allowing any and every thought to sweep in, unpack its suitcase, and set up housekeeping. Soon the flag of human reason is flying over the castle of the mind.

Forgetting that we are to love God with all the mind, as well as with all the heart and soul (Matt. 22:37), many modern conservative Christians treat the mind like an unwanted relative. They emphasize the spiritual, experience, faith. But the mind does matter. Earl Radmacher said, "Right living begins with right thinking. And right thinking begins with thinking right about God."[1]

Through the renewing of our minds, we are transformed (Rom. 12:2). The mind is like a computer: you feed it facts, it processes them, and it comes up with an answer. From the moment of conception we begin receiving facts, impressions, influences—data—upon which we base our decisions. Our programming determines our thinking.

Years ago when computers first became common, a man from IBM tried to explain to me how they worked. He was in awe of the machines, speaking with intense enthusiasm about all of the wonderful things they could do. Then he said, "But you have to remember GIGO."

"What's that?" I asked.

"Garbage in, garbage out," he replied. "The computer is at the mercy of its programming. It computes on the basis of information received. If you enter the wrong data, its computation is going to be wrong. Garbage in, garbage out."

The same principle applies to our minds. Throughout our lives, we have received a lot of false information; therefore, many of our actions are wrong because of faulty programming. Our minds need to be renewed, furnished with new and true information. Then based on this new programming, this new way of thinking, our lives will be transformed. The new data come from the Word of God; as we feed on the Word of God, our thinking changes, and we begin to act right because we think right.

When Israel reached Kadesh-barnea and was preparing to cross into the promised land, Moses first sent twelve men to spy out the land. Upon returning, ten of the spies reported that everything said about the land was true. But there was one thing that hadn't been said—there were giants in the land, and in their eyes the Israelites were just grasshoppers. No way could Israel conquer the land. Well, if you think like a grasshopper, you'll act like one.

Two of the spies, Joshua and Caleb, came to a different

conclusion. True, the land was filled with giants, but they were just bread for God's people. Take along some peanut butter and we'll make sandwiches of them. Joshua and Caleb saw what the others saw, but they had additional data—God. Taking God into account, Israel would have no problem taking the land. Joshua and Caleb had renewed minds.

The tenth chapter of Acts furnishes a good illustration of renewing the mind. God was ready to bring the first Gentile, Cornelius, to Christ. Cornelius was ready to be saved, so God had to ready a witness to share the gospel with him. And whom did God choose? The one apostle who didn't believe salvation was for the Gentiles! Don't tell me God doesn't have a sense of humor. But Peter never would have gone to a Gentile's house in his present condition. His mind was thinking wrongly and needed to be renewed, reprogrammed.

While Cornelius, at God's bidding, was sending a man to fetch Peter, Peter fell asleep on a rooftop and had a vision: "He saw heaven opened and something like a large sheet being let down to earth by its four corners. It contained all kinds of four-footed animals, as well as reptiles of the earth and birds of the air. Then a voice told him, 'Get up, Peter. Kill and eat'" (Acts 10:11–13). But Peter refused, saying that he had never eaten anything impure or unclean. "The voice spoke to him a second time, 'Do not call anything impure that God has made clean'" (v. 15). That happened three times. And then there was a knock at the door. It was Cornelius's messengers seeking Peter. You know the rest of the story. Peter went to Cornelius's house, against the laws of the Jews, and won the first Gentile·

to Christ. Later when Peter was reprimanded for his actions, he defended himself by relating his vision on the rooftop. After his mind had been reprogrammed by the word of God, he thought differently and was transformed.

Meditating, musing, humming on the providence of God will renew our minds, our way of thinking, and thus transform our lives, especially when it comes to surviving friendly fire.

THE BENEFITS OF MEDITATING ON GOD'S PROVIDENCE

Faith must have a faulty memory because God constantly warned His people of the danger of forgetting and exhorted them to remember. When they were about to enter the promised land, God said, "Remember how the LORD your God led you all the way in the desert these forty years" (Deut. 8:2). And in verse 11, He warned, "Be careful that you do not forget the LORD your God." And in verse 18: "But remember the LORD your God, for it is he who gives you the ability to produce wealth."

In David's psalm of thanksgiving in 1 Chronicles 16, he asserted, "Remember the wonders he has done, his miracles, and the judgments he pronounced" (v. 12). "Remember to extol his work," we're told in Job 36:24. During a stressful time in his life, David said,

I will remember the deeds of the LORD;
yes, I will remember your miracles of long ago.

I will meditate on all your works
   and consider all your mighty deeds. (Ps. 77:11–12)

And nearly every church I enter has these words carved on the Communion table: "Do This in Remembrance of Me."

A BOOK OF REMEMBRANCE

It is easy to forget the goodness of God. When God delivers us, we imagine that we will never forget such a mercy, but a week, a month, a year later when another crisis arises, we go through the same hand-wringing exercises, wondering why God has abandoned us. Like some unwanted mongrel, we have been taken into the woods and dropped.

That's why I advise keeping a book of remembrance. Paper is cheaper than brains. Keep a journal in which you record every providential happening of God in your life, and then when you find yourself in desperate straits, go back to the journal and once again remember God's faithfulness. Written memorials secure you against the failure of memory. Read and reread this book, especially during times of trials. Was I ever this distressed before? Is this the first time God seems to have forgotten me? Let me consider the ways of old, the years of ancient times, as Asaph did in Psalm 77:5: "I thought about the former days, the years of long ago."

"O fill your hearts with the thoughts of Him and His ways. If a single act of Providence is so ravishing and transporting, what would many such be, if they were presented together to the view of the soul! If one star is so beautiful to behold, what is a constellation!"[2]

One of the first and greatest benefits of meditating on God's providence is that it quickens the memory, shoring up the walls of a faith collapsing during a time of testing.

GIVING THANKS

This leads to another valuable benefit to you, the believer. It enables you to "give thanks in all circumstances, for this is God's will for you in Christ Jesus" (1 Thess. 5:18). Paul admonished the Ephesians to be "always giving thanks to God the Father for everything, in the name of our Lord Jesus Christ" (Eph. 5:20).

Several years ago I was preaching in California, and after the service a young brother and sister came up to me and introduced themselves. Then the brother said to his sister, "What do you think?"

"I think it's him," the sister said.

The brother said, "Excuse me, you don't know what we're talking about. A few months ago our mother was in a bad car accident. Three others riding with her were killed. She lingered about two weeks. We—my sister and I—were very bitter and angry at what had happened. Our mother told us they had been listening to a tape at the time of the accident. She said we should locate the car and see if the tape was still intact and listen to it.

"We found the tape. It had written on it 'Give Thanks in

Everything.' That's all. No name of the speaker. We listened to that tape for the two weeks that my mother lay dying, and we learned to give thanks to God. It transformed our lives, and when she died, we experienced great victory and peace. But we never knew who the preacher was. Tonight, listening to you, my sister and I recognized your voice. We believe you were the preacher on that tape. Did you ever preach a sermon on that subject?"

I was happy to confess that I had, and we had a wonderful time rejoicing over what God had done in their lives through the act of thanksgiving.

Personally I think it is impossible to survive friendly fire without learning the art of giving God thanks in everything. And the providence of God makes it possible.

Don't get me wrong. I don't mean we ought to jump up and down with joy and thanksgiving when something bad happens, saying, "Thank You, Lord, that my mother was killed." But in the midst of that tragedy we must give thanks to God, knowing that He is a providential God in control of every facet of our lives, and whatever happens He will work it out to our good. In giving God thanks we are acknowledging—and accepting—that our God is in sovereign control of all that happens and that He will fit it into His eternal purpose.

A woman in our church spoke with me frequently about some grievance, usually about how her husband or somebody else was treating her. She was a bitter and unpleasant woman to be around. One day she came to my office for a counseling session, and as she sat down, I handed her my tape

"Thankful in Everything." "Before we talk," I said, "I want you to go home and listen to this tape. Then we'll talk." Several days passed before she called me: "I was angry when you gave me that tape and told me to leave. I felt you were just dismissing me. But I've listened to that tape several times now, and I want to thank you, or thank God, for it. I don't think I'll need to come in." In the following months I watched as her relationship with her husband, her children, and her friends improved dramatically. She actually became a happy woman.

Another benefit is that musing on the past faithfulness of God will stir up a spiritually dull heart, like fresh water on wilting flowers. The very root of praise is remembering His mercies and favors, His deliverances and answers to our prayers. In times of severest drought we will find there a well of assurance that never dries up.

MEDITATE ON THE MAJESTY OF GOD'S PROVIDENCE

God's providence is vast, embracing all His creation. Consider Paul's words in Colossians: "For by him [Christ] all things were created: things in heaven and on earth, visible and invisible, whether thrones or powers or rulers or authorities; all things were created by him and for him. He is before all things, and in him all things hold together" (1:16–17). The apostle did not shrink from saying that *all* things are under His control. Not only is He the power behind creation; He is the preserver of it—"in him all things hold together." He preserves the cohesion in the universe. He is eternity's glue. His arm upholds the universe, and if it were removed, all things would fade into their original nonexistence. He struck a match on the rock of omnipotence and set the sun on fire; He drapes the moon in silver beauty and guides the planets on their course, keeping them from collision and disorder, making this world a cosmos instead of a chaos.

And if He can hold the universe together, I believe He can hold our lives together. Only when Jesus is not preeminent in our hearts do our lives tend to come apart.

MEDITATE ON THE MYSTERIES OF GOD'S PROVIDENCE

Paul expressed for all of us a certain frustration with God: "Oh, the depth of the riches of the wisdom and knowledge of God! How unsearchable his judgments, and his paths beyond tracing out!" (Rom. 11:33). Even David with all his knowledge of God was compelled to say, "Your justice [is] like the great deep" (Ps. 36:6).

Mankind has always grappled with the mystery of God's doings. Jeremiah's frustration was obvious in his comments:

You are always righteous, O LORD,
    when I bring a case before you.
Yet I would speak with you about your justice:
    Why does the way of the wicked prosper?
    Why do all the faithless live at ease?
You have planted them, and they have taken root;
    they grow and bear fruit.

111

> You are always on their lips
>> but far from their hearts. (JER. 12:1–2)

I find myself saying with Jeremiah, "Yes, Lord, what about all that? I, too, would like to talk to You about Your justice." God's ways are mysterious because they confuse us.

1. For many things that happen we can discern no reason except that it pleases God. When God took Jeremiah to the potter's house to give the prophet his message, He spoke of the clay marred in the potter's hand: "So the potter formed it into another pot, shaping it *as seemed best to him*" (Jer. 18:4, emphasis added). As seemed best to him! Does that answer satisfy us? What seems to be confusion to us is order to God.

2. God never seems to announce His providential action. Most of His acts are silent and unknown. He hides His works by removing the results far from human observation. You are familiar with this one, aren't you?

> Those who sow in tears
>> will reap with songs of joy.
> He who goes out weeping,
>> carrying seed to sow,
> will return with songs of joy,
>> carrying sheaves with him. (Ps. 126:5–6)

But for us there is space between sowing and reaping big enough for an eternity to fit into comfortably. But then if we, like God, could see the end from the beginning, there would be no need of faith, and our afflictions would not be trials.

3. Adding to the mystery is the fact that God often uses instruments that go against our common sense. As we have already seen, God brought His people out of Babylon by the power of a worshiper of the sun, Cyrus. Would you have used a raven to feed Elijah? Would you have chosen a boy named Jeremiah to pull down, destroy, and build up kingdoms? Would you have birthed the Messiah in a stable? Would you have chosen a band of uneducated men to carry your saving message to the world? God chose a persecutor to become a great apostle and Scripture writer. He rejected the seven elder sons of Jesse and placed the crown of a kingdom on a little shepherd boy. God chose "the foolish things of the world to shame the wise; God chose the weak things of the world to shame the strong. He chose the lowly things of this world and the despised things—and the things that are not—to nullify the things that are, so that no one may boast before him" (1 Cor. 1:27–29).

4. Mysterious and confusing are His ways because at times He works slowly and at other times, swiftly. It took twenty-four years for Joseph to be reconciled with his brothers, but in less than twenty-four hours Daniel was delivered from the lions' den. The Babylonian captivity stretched into seventy years, but in just a few minutes, Shadrach, Meshach, and Abednego were out of the fiery furnace. God takes His time and is never hurried. One day is with the Lord as a thousand years (I've had days like that) and a thousand years as one day. The words of

the book of Hebrews are words to us: "So do not throw away your confidence; it will be richly rewarded. You need to persevere so that when you have done the will of God, you will receive what he has promised" (10:35–36).

MEDITATE ON THE MERCIES OF GOD'S PROVIDENCE

God's providence allows us fresh discoveries of God's grace and wisdom toward His people. Do you remember Paul's words to the Corinthians? He was describing a painful experience in Asia; actually he was defending himself against some in the church who were murmuring against him, questioning his honesty, and raising doubts about his authenticity as an apostle. He said, "We do not want you to be uninformed, brothers, about the hardships we suffered in the province of Asia. We were under great pressure, far beyond our ability to endure, so that we despaired even of life. Indeed, in our hearts we felt the sentence of death" (2 Cor. 1:8–9). How could God put His faithful servant through such an ordeal? Or, if it makes us feel better, how could God allow Paul to go through that? Paul answered our question: "This happened that we might not rely on ourselves but on God, who raises the dead. He has delivered us from such a deadly peril, and he will deliver us. On him we have set our hope that he will continue to deliver us" (vv. 9–10).

What mercies Paul found through this providence! He learned not to trust in himself (not an easy lesson to learn), and born into his heart was the assurance that in future afflictions, God would deliver him.

One of God's toughest tasks is to teach us that His grace is sufficient. Usually it takes a "thorn" experience for us to discover this. I've spoken in previous books about the death of our son, my physical and emotional problems, and my wife's illnesses. In those afflictions I often despaired of life and felt the sentence of death within me. When my son took his life, he also took mine. But God, in His mercy, gave me a new life for which I would take nothing.

To me, the greatest evidence of the mercy of God in providence is that mystery of all mysteries, the cross of Christ. Many Christians feel that we lost more in the Fall than we gained at the Cross. But the truth is, we are far better off with the salvation we have in Christ than we would have been had sin never rubbed its muddy feet in our paradise. We have a salvation that fascinates even the angels of God. Peter said that they long to look into these things that Christ has obtained for us (1 Peter 1:12). Even the unsinning angels, who live in the very presence of God Himself, do not possess the abundance of mercies you and I do through Jesus Christ.

PART 3

RETURNING FRIENDLY FIRE

†

Though justice be thy plea, consider this,
That in the course of justice none of us
Should see salvation: we do pray for mercy,
And that same prayer doth teach us all to render
The deeds of mercy.
— SHAKESPEARE

There is a hard law . . . that when a deep injury is done to us,
we never recover until we forgive.
— ALAN PATON

It is the person who most knows himself liable to
fall that will be most
ready to overlook any offenses from his fellow man.
— ALEXANDER AULD

CHAPTER 11

I KNEW YOU WERE GOING TO SAY THAT

Forgive.

A while back I was driving down a highway near our house, and as I came to an overpass, I noticed a message spray-painted on its side: "Kickapoo, forgive me."

I drove that same road a few days later, and when I came to the overpass, I saw that the earlier message had been painted over with one word: "Forgiven."

That's a beautiful word, *forgiven*. No sweeter sound can come from one you have injured than the word *forgiven*. We all need it. We all seek it.

Although it is contrary to our fallen nature and viewed as wimpish by our vigilante society, the subject of forgiveness was preeminent in the teachings of Jesus. When He taught the disciples to pray, He gave them the Model Prayer, commonly called the Lord's Prayer. The prayer is made up of six petitions:

1. "Hallowed be your name."
2. "Your kingdom come."
3. "Your will be done."
4. "Give us today our daily bread."
5. "Forgive us our debts, as we also have forgiven our debtors."
6. "Lead us not into temptation."

This prayer (Matt. 6:9–13) is a blueprint for all our prayers. Each prayer is to be built according to these specifications. But having given us the six petitions, Jesus felt it necessary to reiterate one of them. Which one? I would have thought "Hallowed be your name" or "Your kingdom come" or "Your will be done." But it was none of those. The petition that Jesus went back over with a highlighter was the one on forgiveness. In the following verses He said, "For if you forgive men when they sin against you, your heavenly Father will also forgive you. *But if you do not forgive men their sins, your Father will not forgive your sins*" (Matt. 6:14–15, emphasis added).

He said to His disciples, "When you stand praying, if you hold anything against anyone, forgive him, so that your Father in heaven may forgive you your sins" (Mark 11:25). In His preaching, teaching, and parables Jesus again and again emphasized forgiveness as essential to maintaining our fellowship with God. The Sermon on the Mount contains a whole section on how we should suffer patiently when wronged (Matt. 5:21–48). Forgiveness was what Jesus was all about. It was the purpose of the Incarnation. Even while He was dying on the cross, His mind was on forgiveness, not revenge: "Father, forgive them, for they do not know what they are doing" (Luke 23:34).

In this Jesus has left us an example, that we should follow in His steps: "When they hurled their insults at him, he did not retaliate; when he suffered, he made no threats" (1 Peter 2:23). So Paul could say, "Be kind and compassionate to one another, forgiving each other, just as in Christ God forgave you" (Eph. 4:32). In Christ we have become new persons, and we must put on the clothes of a Christlike life, a part of which includes bearing "with each other" and forgiving "whatever grievances you may have against another. Forgive as the Lord forgave you" (Col. 3:13).

As John MacArthur notes, "God is the consummate forgiver. And we depend every day on His ongoing forgiveness for our sins. The least we can do is emulate His forgiveness in our dealings with one another."[1] It is unthinkable that one who has received mercy should not, in return, dispense mercy. We are never more like Christ than when we forgive those who have sinned against us.

WHAT IS FORGIVENESS?

The most common New Testament word for "forgiveness" is *aphesis*. The noun occurs fifteen times and the verb about forty times. It conveys the idea of "sending away," "letting go," "releasing," and "leaving." In the Old Testament, after the high priest placed his hands on the head of a goat and confessed the sins of the people, thus transferring their sins to the goat, he "let it go." It was taken into the wilderness and left. The sins of the people had been sent away: "The goat will carry on itself all their sins to a solitary place; and the man shall release it in the desert" (Lev. 16:22). It presents a perfect picture of Christ bearing our sins upon Himself and taking them away.

When Jesus appeared while John the Baptist was baptizing in the river Jordan, John pointed to Jesus and cried, "Look, the Lamb of God, who takes away the sin of the world!" (John 1:29). He could have said, "who takes away the *sinners* of the world," but not so. God destroys not the sinner, but the sin. He takes away not the offender, but the offense. By one stroke of lightning, He could have taken away the sinners, but it required the blood of His heart to take away the sin. To make the world, He had only to speak a word; but to save the world, He had to crucify His own Son. John knew that one day the sins of the world would be placed on the head of this, the true Lamb, and He would bear them away.

And so we stand with our hands upon the head of Jesus; He is standing in our place. We come to the cross and realize that He was wounded for our transgressions and bruised for our iniquities.

> Not all the blood of beasts
> On Jewish altars slain
> Could give the guilty conscience peace
> Or wash away the stain.

But Christ, the heavenly Lamb,
Takes all our sins away;
A sacrifice of nobler name,
And richer blood than they.

My faith would lay her hand
On that meek head of thine,
While as a penitent I stand,
And there confess my sin.

Believing, we rejoice
To feel the curse remove;
We bless the Lamb with cheerful voice,
And trust His bleeding love.

(ISAAC WATTS)

For us, to forgive someone is to let go of a grudge, to abandon our desire for revenge, to release that person from obligation, to dismiss our demand for repentance on his part.

But there is an important difference between our forgiveness and God's. When God forgives, He absolves from guilt. Only God can do that. Our forgiveness does not absolve from guilt, but opens the way for the restoration of fellowship, removing the barrier to reconciliation.

We must always remember that forgiveness and reconciliation are not the same things. Lewis Drummond writes, "Forgiveness is the removal of a barrier. There is a tendency in Christian circles to us the word 'forgiveness' so broadly as to denote the *total* experience of human reconciliation with God. In the Bible, however, forgiveness is primarily the removal of barriers which sin erects against fellowship with God. Thus it is the precondition of reconciliation in its fullness."[2] We are to forgive the offender; that is unilateral forgiveness, of which I will speak more later. But if the offender does not accept the forgiveness or respond to it in a reconciling way, there can be no restoration to fellowship. You may forgive someone and yet that someone may not change his attitudes or feelings toward you. In his book *Life Lines*, Forrest Church speaks of forgiveness: "When we forgive someone we don't change them, but ourselves. We liberate ourselves from all obligations to continuing bitterness. This doesn't reverse the past. But it changes the present and the future."[3] We are not responsible for the other person's response; we are responsible only to forgive.

And so we forgive. Why? Because others repent and make amends? No. We forgive for the simple reason God has forgiven us. And the unforgiving Christian is a Christian who does not fully appreciate the operation of grace in his life. We must forgive not because the person deserves it, but because God demands it. The offender's attitude or continued actions have not a single thing to do with whether or not we forgive him. We forgive because we are forgiven. It is a must.

It would be so much easier to forgive if others would ask for it, wouldn't it? Just flat-out forgiving is difficult, almost impossible. Why? There are many barriers to forgiveness, but I believe the greatest is that we do not fully understand that we, too, are sinners needing forgiveness. There is, John MacArthur says, "a natural, sinful tendency for all of us to minimize our own sins and magnify the blame of others—to treat ourselves with mercy and demand retribution against others. If we would only learn to be more repulsed by our own sin than we are at the wrongs of others, we would be well on the road to spiritual health."[4] And yet all of us are guilty. None of us would dare ask the question Christ asked, "Which of you convicts Me of sin?" (John 8:46 NKJV). We see the sin of others, but fail to see our own sin. In forgiving another, we are simply giving what we ourselves desperately need. Dietrich Bonhoeffer wrote,

> The most experienced observer of humanity knows less of the human heart than the Christian who lives at the foot of the cross of Christ. No psychology knows that people perish only through sin and are saved only through the cross of Christ. Anyone who has seen the meaning of the cross but for a moment is shocked by the godlessness of the world and by the awesomeness of his own sins; he will no longer be shocked by the sins of his sisters and brothers in Christ. The spirit of judgment is cut off at the roots.[5]

I think the reason Jesus reemphasized the petition on forgiveness in the Model Prayer is that He knew this to be the most important and the hardest part of all. And it is. C. S. Lewis observed, "Everyone says forgiveness is a lovely idea until he has someone to forgive."

So before we can forgive, we must be forgiven. Before we can restore a sinning brother to fellowship, we must make certain that our fellowship with God and one another is right. To be sinned against should be a reminder of our sin and our need of forgiveness. Let's talk about that.

CHAPTER 12

MAINTAINING OUR FELLOWSHIP

When a person is born, he enters into a relationship.

I was born in nineteen hundred and none-of-your-business. I was born to Cecil and Eunice Dunn. Cecil Dunn was my father, and I was his son. That was our relationship. That relationship was automatic and required no maintenance. No matter what I did, I was still his son. He was stuck with me and I was stuck with him. I could have changed my name and fled to the darkest jungle and never set eyes on him again. But that wouldn't have dissolved the relationship. He could have disowned me in a court of law, but I would still be his flesh-and-blood son.

In the same way, when we are saved, born again, we enter into a relationship with God. He is our Father and we are His children. That relationship is automatic and requires no maintenance. I may be a rebellious and disobedient child. Like the prodigal son, I may flee to a far country, but even in the pigpen of disobedience, I am His son.

Birth establishes a relationship, and it creates a fellowship. The extent to which I enjoy the relationship is determined by the quality of the fellowship. When everything was right between Dad and me, I enjoyed our relationship, especially at Christmas. But there were many times when I didn't get a kick out of being my father's son, especially when I got a kick out of it because of my disobedience (no, my dad never kicked me, but I became very familiar with his belt). Didn't you ever say when you were a kid, "I wish I had different parents"? You said that because the fellowship between you and your parents left something to be desired. To enjoy the privileges of sonship (for example, taking the family car out on Saturday nights), I had to maintain a proper fellowship.

The same thing is true with God. The extent to which I enjoy my relationship with the Father is determined by our fellowship. In the far country, the prodigal was still the father's son, but he could not benefit from that relationship. He was penniless, friendless, and starving. It was only when he returned to the father in repentance and confession that he received the best robe, shoes for his feet, and a ring on his finger. The boy was right when he said, "How many of my father's hired servants have food to spare, and here I am starving to death!" (Luke 15:17). There are more joy and benefit in being a hired servant than in being a disobedient child on the lam. The most miserable person in the world is a Christian out of fellowship with God.

First and foremost, above all other things, the Christian must maintain his fellowship with God and the family. And this is the burden of the apostle John's first epistle: "We proclaim to you what we have seen and heard, so that you also may have fellowship with us. And our fellowship is with the Father and with his Son, Jesus Christ. We write this to make our joy complete" (1 John 1:3–4).

Notice the close connection between joy and fellowship. Some years ago a pastor asked me to speak at the church's adult Sweetheart Banquet. I knew that a couple in the church was giving him and the church all kinds of problems. We gathered for the banquet; everybody was having a good time with the singing and joke telling and acting crazy. After a while I leaned over to the pastor and said, "I bet I can tell you which couple is giving you all the trouble in your church."

"You think so?" he said. "Which one?"

I mentioned a certain table and said, "He's wearing a blue suit with a gray tie, and she's wearing a flowery blue dress with a red corsage."

He was amazed. "You're right. How did you know?"

"Well, we've been sitting here for about forty minutes and everybody's having a great time. But that couple haven't cracked a smile the whole time."

The extent to which we enjoy our relationship is determined by our fellowship.

John said he was writing to those Christians, his little children, so that they might have fellowship. He had a message that would show them how to maintain that fellowship.

And what was that message? "This is the message we have heard from him and declare to you: God is light; in him there is no darkness at all. If we claim to have fellowship with him yet walk in the darkness, we lie and do not live by the truth" (1 John 1:5–6).

Light. Darkness. In John's epistle, the former means purity and the latter, sin. God is Light (pure), and if we want to walk in fellowship with Him, we cannot walk in darkness (sin). In other words, the only thing that can mar our fellowship with God and one another (v. 7) is sin. Therefore, we must constantly deal with the sin problem in our lives to maintain fellowship.

THERE MUST BE A CONSCIOUSNESS OF THE SIN IN OUR LIVES

We are never as spiritual as we think we are. In verse 8, John wrote, "If we claim to be without sin, we deceive ourselves and the truth is not in us," and in verse 10, "If we claim we have not sinned, we make him out to be a liar and his word has no place in our lives."

Notice in verse 8, John used the word *sin*, a noun, and in verse 10, he used the word *sinned*, a verb. *Sin*, the noun, refers to the *principle* of sin in our lives, the old nature. *Sinned*, the verb, refers to the *practice* of sin. If we say that we are sinless, that the principle of sin is not in us, "we deceive ourselves." I wrote in the margin of my Bible, "And no one else!"

When I was a teenager, my pastor related this incident.

He was walking down the main street of our town and ran into another pastor. His eight-year-old boy was with him. In the course of their conversation, the other pastor said, "You know, brother, I have received the second blessing. The old sin nature has been eradicated and I don't sin anymore. Not for three years now." But boys will be boys, and his eight-year-old son looked up at my pastor and said, "Dontcha believe it."

If I should say that I have no sin, my wife, my children, and my friends wouldn't be deceived—neither would God. I would deceive only myself. If I say I have not sinned, I am making God out to be a liar because He has said that I have. Remember, John was writing to fellow believers.

A consciousness of my sinfulness indicates that I am walking in the light. It's hard to see dirt in the dark; you must bring it to the light. God is the Light, and the closer we are to Him, the more obvious becomes the sin in our lives. In my religious tradition we have what we call revival meetings, and at the end of the message we call for Christians to come to the altar and get right with God. Through the years I've noticed that the first ones at the altar are usually some of the most godly people in the church. It is easy for them to see their sin because they live in the light.

Vance Havner tells of a prayer meeting in which the leader said, "Let's get on our knees and confess our sins." All but one did. The leader said to the solitary saint, "Get down on your knees and confess your sins."

"Why," the man said, "I can't think of a single sin."

"Well, get down there and guess at it!"

He did, and he guessed right the very first time.

THERE MUST BE A CONFESSION
OF OUR SINS

John wrote, "If we confess our sins, he is faithful and just and will forgive us our sins and purify us from all unrighteousness" (1 John 1:9). If we confess, He will forgive; if we do not confess, He will not forgive. But someone says, "That doesn't sound right. If we are saved, haven't we already been forgiven all our sins? When Christ died, didn't He take all our sins away, past, present, and future?"

This thinking, which is correct, has led many to teach that we, as believers, do not need to confess our sins because they have already been forgiven. Continuing to confess our sins would be denying the work of the Cross.

But 1 John was written to believers, not unbelievers. John called his readers "my little children" and "brothers." And he said plainly that we are to confess our sins, and that when we do so, God will forgive them. How do we explain this?

Remember, we're talking about fellowship, not relationship. As far as our relationship as children of God, we do not need to confess our sins to maintain that relationship. But fellowship is another matter. If I want to stay in fellowship with God, I must confess my sins.

An incident in the life of Jesus throws light on this matter. The Lord was in the Upper Room with His disciples, and suddenly He got up from the supper table and began washing the feet of His disciples. When He came to Peter, the disciple said, "Lord, are you going to wash my feet?" (John 13:6). Jesus replied, "Right now you don't know what I'm doing, but later on you will understand." Peter drew back and said, "You will never wash my feet!" But Jesus said, "Unless I wash you, you have no part with me" (v. 8). "Well, then," Peter said, "that being the case, don't wash my feet only but also my hands and my head." Jesus answered, "A person who has had a bath needs only to wash his feet; his whole body is clean" (v. 10).

In those days people wore sandals, and few of the streets were paved. Let's suppose I rise one morning, take a bath, dress, and then decide to visit my friend Sam. When I get to his house, my feet are covered with dust. I don't say to Sam, "Let me use your bathtub; I got dirty walking down here." Sam would say, "You don't need to take a bath; only your feet are dirty. Here — use this basin of water by the door and wash the dust from your feet." It was improper to walk into another's house with dirty feet. Before you could enjoy fellowship with your friend, you must first wash your feet.

When we first trusted Christ as Savior, we got the bath, cleansed from head to toe. But in our daily walk, the dust of the world accumulates on our feet, and there must be daily cleansing if we are to come into the Lord's presence and have fellowship. That's why the word *confess* is written in a tense indicating continual confession.

What does it mean to confess our sins? The Greek word

John used for "confess" is *homologeo* (to speak the same thing, to say again, to assent, to agree with). When we confess our sins, we say the same thing about them that God says. God says, "This thing is sin." I say, "I agree." When we confess to men, we tell them something they don't know. But when we confess to God, we don't tell Him something He doesn't already know; we simply agree with God's estimate of the thing.

That's not easy for us to do. We prefer to call it something else. A few years ago a memo was circulated among the federal offices of the government. In part it said, "We no longer use the words *waste* and *fraud*. We use the phrase 'managerial oversight.'" That sounds better, doesn't it? Once when I had finished a sermon on gossip, a woman came to me and said, "I wouldn't call what I do gossip. I just have a talkative nature."

"Well, that's bad news," I said. "The Bible says that God will forgive sins like gossip, but nowhere does He say He forgives a talkative nature."

This is one of our biggest problems. We prefer to use the word *habit* or the phrase "personal idiosyncrasy." But a rose by any other name smells the same. The reason some of us lack the power to overcome besetting sins is that we refuse to label them *sins*.

So I must ask myself, "Are God and I in total agreement about every issue in my life?" If I am not, then I am walking in darkness.

Again notice the apostle used the plural, *sins*. That's

more than one. We often pray, "Lord, forgive us our sins." But that isn't confessing our sins. The only way we can confess sins, more than one, is by naming them. Now I'm not advocating making a sin list, but when we come to confession, we need to name them one by one as the Spirit brings them to our minds. "Lord, I lost my temper today. I said some unkind words about a friend. I entertained some unworthy thoughts today." In this way we are confronting our sins rather than lumping them in a garbage bag and tossing them in the alley.

PUBLIC CONFESSION OF SINS?

Whenever we talk about confession of sins, the question of public confession invariably comes up: Should we publicly confess our sins to one another? Often James 5:16 is quoted as a basis for such confession: "Therefore confess your sins to each other and pray for each other so that you may be healed." The determining word here is *therefore*, which unmistakably connects it to the context of sickness caused by sin and calling for the elders to pray. The confession of which James spoke is the confession of those sins that have brought about the sickness. "And pray for each other so that you may be healed," not so that you may be forgiven. This verse is not a text for public confession of sin.

However, many times when God visits His people with renewal or revival, there is public confession of sin. In public confession two guidelines must be observed. First, it must be *spontaneous*. People must not be forced, berated, or intimidated into public confession of their sins. Demanding public confession is not scriptural. Second, public confession must be *selective*. We must not indict other people by name or drag into the light the shameful things that are done in darkness. I have been in some meetings where the public confession was not only embarrassing but downright tempting to the flesh. A good rule is that the confession should be only as wide as the knowledge of the sin. If the entire church knows a man has been living a wicked life, he can confess publicly to that kind of light—without going into salacious details. What is private should be kept private, confessed only to God.

THERE MUST BE CLEANSING
FROM OUR SINS

When we confess our sins, God does two things: first, He forgives us; second, He cleanses us. "If we confess our sins, he is faithful and just to forgive us our sins, *and to cleanse us from all unrighteousness*" (1 John 1:9 KJV, emphasis added). Whatever God forgives, He also cleanses. Forgiveness and cleansing (purification) are not the same things. When we sin, not only is there the offense against God, but there is the stain left by the sin—and it must be cleansed.

It's Sunday morning and his mother has gotten little Jimmy all dressed up in his Sunday duds. An angel, he is. But it's not yet time to leave, so he asks his mother if he can go outside and play. Mom says, yes, but don't get dirty.

In a few minutes little Jimmy creeps back into the house, trying to avoid Mom. But she sees him and nearly chokes with unbelief. Little Jimmy is covered from head to toe in dirt and mud. He knows he is a doomed little boy. He is about to receive the severest spanking of his life.

So he pleads. Like all little boys, he knows how to handle these situations. He pushes out his lower lip, forces a tear out of his big brown eyes, and says, "Oh, Mommy, I'm sorry, I'm so sorry. Please don't spank me!"

Now no self-respecting mother could turn a deaf ear to such a plea. After all, he is a little angel.

"Okay," Mommy says, "I forgive you. I'm not going to spank you. Now get out of those clothes and climb into the bathtub."

But little Jimmy just stands there, his eyes cast down, his thumb in his mouth.

"Jimmy, I told you I wasn't going to spank you. Now get into the tub."

But little Jimmy doesn't move.

"Jimmy," his mother says in exasperation, "what's wrong with you? Get into the bathtub so we can wash all that mud off."

Still studying the floor and sucking his thumb, little Jimmy, the little angel, mutters, "I like the mud."

Jimmy wanted to be forgiven, but not cleansed. He wanted to avoid punishment for his sin, but he liked his sin and didn't want to part with it. Does that sound familiar? Many of us want forgiveness so God won't spank us, but we're unwilling to let Him wash away the dirt. But God does not forgive without cleansing.

And when He forgives our sins, He even washes away the stain that the sin left on our lives. "He cleanses us from *all* unrighteousness." The attitude of repentance and confession is such that God cleanses us even from the sins of which we are unaware. He takes away all unrighteousness so that we stand spotless in His sight.

There is an interesting—and puzzling—sequence in 1 John 1:7: "If we walk in the light, as he is in the light, we have fellowship with one another, and the blood of Jesus, his Son, purifies us from all sin." The arrangement seems to be wrong. Shouldn't John have said first that the blood cleanses us from all sin, then we walk in the light and have fellowship with one another? But I know John can't be wrong, so the sequence must be correct.

First, he said, "If we walk in the light, as he is in the light." In other words, God doesn't forgive sin in the dark! We can't remain in our darkness and expect God to cleanse us. We must leave the darkness and come to the light. That's repentance.

Then, he spoke of our fellowship with one another. Only then does the blood of Jesus cleanse us from all sin. The message is clear: you can't be wrong with your fellow believer and right with God. You come to God in repentance, make things right (as much as it is possible for you to do so) with your brother, then the blood of Jesus cleanses you. You can confess all you want, you can plead for forgiveness until the proverbial cows come home, but if you refuse to be in fellowship with your brethren, you're wasting your time.

HOW GOD FORGIVES

Listen to John as he spoke assuring words: "My little children, these things write I unto you, that ye sin not [that's the ideal]. And if any man sin [that's the reality], we have an advocate with the Father, Jesus Christ the righteous: and he is the propitiation [covering] for our sins: and not for ours only, but also for the sins of the whole world" (1 John 2:1–2 KJV). Propitiation means the satisfaction of God's demand for justice.

Advocate is a fancy word for a lawyer. It means "one who stands by your side and pleads your case." Now this is a good lawyer. For one thing, His Father is the Judge! He is "righteous," so He is in good standing with the court, and He pleads not our innocence but His blood. And He has never lost a case.

Years ago, we decided to turn our living room, small and unused, into a study so I could move my library from the church to the house. We hired an inferior—excuse me—an interior decorator to do the job. Before the work began, we sat down and itemized everything to be done and the cost of each item. Then the carpenters went to work—and I use the term loosely. They made a mess of everything. The bookshelves leaned and sagged like a drunk man trying to look respectable but not making it. They had to add extra boards so the shelves would meet at the corners. They convinced me to let them build my desk: "Just as nice as you would buy at a store." When the desk was delivered, I examined it. It was built from leftover bookshelf wood, the drawers were stapled together (I mean the kind of staples you use on paper!), and the first one I pulled open came apart. It was the desk from hell. No way was I going to accept the pile of scrap wood. And I told them so. They removed the desk and never came back, leaving much of the work undone.

A few days later I received a bill from them for the total amount. I sat down with the itemized list and wrote a check for what they had done, even though what they had done was sloppy. The check came to half the original amount.

About a week later the mail dumped the check in my lap with the word UNACCEPTABLE scrawled across it. Accompanying the rejected check was a letter saying they were suing me for the full amount. I had never been sued before. How was that going to look? I could see the headlines: "Local Pastor Sued for Nonpayment."

I worried over that for a few days, then Kaye suggested I see a lawyer. Why didn't I think of that?

When I sat down in the lawyer's office, I told him my tale of woe while he recorded the conversation. When I finished, he clicked off the recorder and stood up. I knew that was the signal for me to leave. But he hadn't told me what to do, so I asked him.

"Nothing," he said.

"But what do I tell them?"

"You've never used a lawyer before, have you?" It was more a statement than a question.

"No," I said.

"Well, Pastor, you don't tell them anything. You don't communicate with them at all. I'll handle everything."

What a relief. But I couldn't resist, so I wrote them a letter: "You'll be hearing from my attorney." That felt good. "My attorney." By the way, my attorney prevailed, but by the time I paid his fee I would have been as well off paying the total amount.

And I have a heavenly Attorney who says to me, "I'll handle everything."

I can see the devil approach the bar of justice and say to God, "Here is an indictment against that preacher of Yours. It is a record of his sins. You Yourself said, 'The wages of sin is death,' and 'The soul that sinneth shall die.' I demand justice. I demand You judge him."

Then suddenly someone stands, surrounded by brilliant light. The angels thrill at the spectacle as Jesus, my Advocate, approaches the bench and rips the indictment from the accuser's hand. He turns to the Judge and says, "Father, everything in this indictment is true. This preacher has sinned. But I demand that he be released from custody." Then He holds up His nail-pierced hands and points to His wounded feet and side. "I do not plead his innocence or justifying circumstances. I plead My blood that was shed in payment for all these sins. The penalty has already been paid in blood."

The devil flees the courtroom, and the verdict is rendered by the Judge: "There is therefore now no condemnation to them which are in Christ Jesus."

CHAPTER 13

A TALE OF
TWO DEBTORS

You are going to be offended.

No matter how hard you try to avoid it, no matter how strong a garrison you build around yourself, somebody will sooner or later breach your defenses and offend you. Jesus said that offenses must come (Matt. 18:7). The only place on earth to find complete peace and harmony is a cemetery. But where there is life, there will be offenses. And the more life there is, that much more the offenses, and that much more must you be ready for them. The faster you drive a car, the tighter the grip you must hold on the steering wheel.

So the question is not what you should do *if* you're offended, but what you should do *when* you're offended. May we have the envelope, please? And the answer is—forgive!

One of the greatest lessons Jesus taught on forgiveness is found in Matthew 18. In this chapter Jesus was expounding the topic of forgiveness.

"Then Peter came to Him [Jesus] and said, 'Lord, how often shall my brother sin against me, and I forgive him? Up to seven times?'" (Matt. 18:21 NKJV). The rabbis said that we should forgive a person three times. Peter was being magnanimous. He took the law, doubled it, and added one for good measure. He probably expected praise from Jesus for such a forgiving heart. But Jesus answered, "I do not say to you, up to seven times, but up to seventy times seven" (v. 22 NKJV). That response must have stunned Peter and the rest—and most likely stuns us, for many of us are eye-for-an-eye Christians. If Jesus had agreed with Peter, you can bet that Peter would have kept track of every one of them.

Then Jesus told a story (He was a great storyteller, you know). Seems there was a servant who owed his master somewhere between $10 and $20 million (where'd a servant get credit like that?), and one day the master called the note. Of course, the servant couldn't pay; his credit cards were maxed out. So the master ordered that the servant and his wife and his children and all that he had be sold to repay the debt. The servant fell at his feet and begged, "Give me a little time and I'll pay back every cent I owe you." If nothing else, he was optimistic.

Surprisingly the master took pity on him, wiped the unpayable debt off the books, and let him go. What exhilaration that man must have felt! That kind of mercy would surely flow through him to others. A man of compassion was born.

But Jesus said, "When that servant went out, he found one of his fellow servants who owed him a hundred denarii.

He grabbed him and began to choke him. 'Pay back what you owe me!' he demanded" (Matt. 18:28).

"His fellow servant fell to his knees and begged him, 'Be patient with me, and I will pay you back'" (v. 29). The same words the first servant had used—they must have sounded familiar. *But he refused!* He had the man thrown into prison until he could pay his debt. Is there something wrong with this picture? He who had been forgiven millions wouldn't forgive a fistful of dollars.

When his fellow servants saw what he had done, they were understandably upset. So they did what anybody would have done—they went to the master and told him everything that had happened.

There is no wrath like that of mercy scorned. "Then the master called the servant in. 'You wicked servant,' he said, 'I canceled all that debt of yours because you begged me to. Shouldn't you have had mercy on your fellow servant just as I had on you?' In anger, his master turned him over to the jailers to be tortured, until he should pay back all he owed. This is how my heavenly Father will treat each of you unless you forgive your brother from your heart" (Matt. 18:32–35).

Which servant do you believe got out of prison first?

Philip Yancey says of verse 35, "I fervently wish those words were not in the Bible, but there they are, from the lips of Christ himself. God has granted us a terrible agency: by denying forgiveness to others, we are in effect determining them unworthy of God's forgiveness, and thus so are we. In some mysterious way, divine forgiveness depends upon us."[1]

145

Instead of forgiving, the wicked servant demanded revenge, payback, to which by law he was entitled. He had every right to throw his debtor in prison. But receiving grace ought to make us willing to give up some of our rights. Instead, we feel that forgiveness is in a sense unfair because it lets our enemy off the hook, and that is foreign to human nature. Jesus pulled no punches in describing the unforgiving servant; He was definitely not being seeker-friendly when He called this servant "wicked." That's a term few of us would use to portray another. But Jesus said that if you and I are unwilling to forgive another, we are "wicked servants." We may preach great sermons, sing in the choir, teach a Bible class, but if we harbor unforgiveness, we are wicked.

So then, how can we escape this wickedness? By forgiveness. "But I have been wronged," you say. "Why then should I forgive?" Let this parable answer that question.

FORGIVENESS IS AN OBLIGATION

Forgiveness is not optional equipment in the Christian life. We have no choice but to forgive, whether we feel like it or not. Forgiveness is not an emotion; it is a decision. Those forgiven must forgive.

Now in truth, no servant would be able to rack up $10 or $20 million in debt. Jesus exaggerated the amount to make it clear: the debt was unpayable. No matter how patient the master might have been, the servant's debt was infinite—as was ours against God. Our debt was infinite and unpayable. But He dipped His towel of mercy in the blood of Jesus and washed the slate clean.

One of my favorite verses is Psalm 103:12: "As far as the east is from the west, so far has he removed our transgressions from us." Have you wondered why He didn't say, "As far as the north is from the south"? That's a long way. I would have settled for that. But He said, "As far as the east is from the west." Why? Well, if you started walking north today and you walked long enough and far enough, you would eventually be walking south. And if you started walking south today and you walked long enough and far enough, you would eventually be walking north. Why? Because north and south meet. There are a North Pole and a South Pole.

If you started walking east today, you could walk for a million years and never walk west. And if you started walking west today, you could walk for a billion years and never walk east. Why? Because east and west never meet. Who ever heard of an East Pole or a West Pole?

Our debt was infinite and so is His forgiveness.

THERAPEUTIC FORGIVENESS VS. GRACE FORGIVENESS

Robert Coles, an eminent psychiatrist, tells of a friend, a devout Roman Catholic, who was dying of cancer. Once he visited his friend and found him quite angry. A priest had visited him to see how he was coping. According to Coles, the priest proceeded in a relentless kind of psychological inquiry. How was the patient "feeling"? How was he "managing" in light of the "stress" he had to "confront"? The patient was enraged by such questions; he wanted to talk about God and God's ways, about Christ and His death, about heaven and hell. But he was repeatedly approached with words and phrases drawn from the vocabulary of popular psychology. The patient told Coles: "He comes with a Roman collar, and offers me psychological banalities as God's Word!" Coles concludes his story by saying,

> There are, of course, many kinds of burdens in this life. I wonder whether the deepest mire, the deepest waters, for America's clergy, not to mention us laymen, may be found in the dreary solipsistic world so many of us have learned to find so interesting: The mind's moods, the various "stages" and "phases" of "human development" or of "dying" all dwelt upon (God save us!) as if Stations of the Cross.[2]

I'm not against psychology and psychiatry. They have their place in our society. But many of the people who are teaching and writing about forgiveness have taken a purely therapeutic tack, saying such things as, "We must forgive if we are to find inner peace and serenity." I'm all for inner peace and serenity, but gaining them is not the primary motivation for forgiveness. As L. Gregory Jones writes,

"Therapeutic language has increasingly distorted the grammar of Christian forgiveness."[3]

In his landmark book *The Triumph of the Therapeutic*, Philip Rieff offered these observations:

> In the emergent culture, a wider range of people will have "spiritual" concerns and be engaged in "spiritual" pursuits. There will be more singing and more listening. People will continue to genuflect and read the Bible, which has long achieved the status of great literature; but no prophet will denounce the rich attire or stop the dancing. There will be more theater, not less, and no Puritan will denounce the stage and draw its curtains. On the contrary, I expect that modern society will mount psychodramas far more frequently than its ancestors mounted miracle plays, with patient-analysts acting out their inner lives, after which they could extemporize the final act as interpretation.[4]

Those words were written in 1967. Quite a prophet.

Grace forgiveness is forgiveness bestowed not because God is trying to make us feel better or to help us achieve inner peace and serenity, but because God in His mercy has forgiven us. One woman told me she was having trouble forgiving another because she felt he "wasn't worthy of my forgiveness." Ah, such arrogance. What is his debt to you, compared to your debt to God? Are any of us worthy of God's forgiveness? We do well not to talk of worthiness.

FORGIVENESS IS AN ACT
OF GRACE, NOT LAW

In other words, forgiveness is unlimited. To Peter's "seven times," Jesus said, "seventy times seven"—490 times. I don't think Jesus meant that literally, or He would have been as legalistic as Peter. My wife passed the 490 mark years ago. No, the phrase means "as often as necessary." As often as necessary to reflect the character of God. As often as necessary to maintain fellowship.

Forgiveness is more than an act. It is a way of life. God provided forgiveness, and still does, so that there might be communion between God and man, between man and man, and with the whole creation. That's why I said earlier that our forgiveness doesn't absolve us from guilt, but removes the barriers for reconciliation. Our focus should be on the restoration of communion. By living in forgiveness we embody the life of Christ.

FORGIVENESS SETS THE
OFFENDER FREE

The wicked servant cast his fellow servant into prison until the debt was paid. That was legal, but it seems stupid to me. It is true that a man in debtors' prison could work for a penny or two a day. But think how much longer it would take him to repay the debt. For many people, being cast into debtors' prison was a life sentence. If a person wasn't free, there was no way he could pay his debt. His freedom was taken away; he was bound for the rest of his life.

When we withhold forgiveness, we put the offender in debtors' prison. We bind him from ever being of any use to us. Perhaps your pastor has offended you, either intentionally or unintentionally. If you do not forgive him, you bind him from ever being a blessing or help to you. He may preach the greatest sermon ever delivered, and everyone in the congregation will be blessed but you. You can focus only on the debt he owes you.

A few years ago, my secretary informed me that one of my pastor friends owed me sixty dollars for some tapes he ordered. "Send him a bill," I said. "I have," she answered. "I've sent a bill every month."

"What does he say?" I asked.

"Nothing."

"Nothing! Doesn't he even acknowledge the bill?"

"No."

I couldn't believe it. He was a friend of mine; I had preached in his church. It wasn't the sixty dollars. If he had said, "Things are tough right now and I can't pay the bill," I would have wiped the debt off the books. But not to say a thing, that's what upset me.

I mumbled a lot about it. Kaye would say, "Why don't you talk to him?" Not my place; besides, I do talk to him every month—with a bill. Every time I heard his name, all I could think was, *He owes me sixty dollars.*

About a year later Kaye and I were attending a convention,

and this fellow spoke at one of the sessions. Everyone said he did a great job. I wouldn't know. All I knew was, he owed me sixty dollars. Later that week, we were sitting in the balcony, and Kaye nudged me. About four aisles down sat my debtor. When the meeting finished, we met in the aisle. I did not acknowledge his presence. But he saw me and grabbed my arm. "Hey, Ron, I'm glad to see you."

"I'm glad to see you too," I lied.

"Listen," he said, "I've owed your office sixty dollars for over a year for some tapes I ordered."

"Is that so?" I said.

"Yeah, and I'm real sorry I haven't paid it. But we've had a rough time financially and I just didn't have the money," he said, reaching into his coat pocket. "But I have the money now and I brought this check with me, hoping I would see you." He presented me with a check for sixty dollars. *Humph*, nothing added for interest. I started to pocket the check, and the Lord said to me, *Give it back*. Of course, that had to be the devil speaking—but I knew it wasn't. I said, "I understand about rough times. Here, take this back and consider it a gift." He did so, thanking me profusely.

He thought it was a gift, but it was a penalty for my unforgiving spirit. It cost me sixty dollars to get right with God.

It is easier to forgive a stranger than a friend. Johann Christoph Arnold tells the story of his friend Pete from Virginia:

Before moving to another state and leaving my business, I had to settle affairs with my partner of ten years. This was complicated by the fact that he and his wife were very close to me; we had been friends for the past fifteen years.

No one would advise me about how best to make an equitable settlement of our business assets. I wanted to be not just fair, but generous. I wanted nothing hanging on my conscience. So I came up with a decision that would give me half of the earnings to the date I left, and leave them the other half, the jobs in progress, and the equity and good will of the business with which to continue. But they saw the whole thing differently and stopped talking to me the day I gave notice. Unfortunately, I had given two months' notice, so the transition was long, silent, and lonely, punctuated only by angry words.

We still had not signed an agreement by the time I left. Lawyers had been brought in by both of us, but they only clouded the waters. I had wanted an outside source to arbitrate the offer, but they fired the arbitrator and sought advice instead from an accountant we had worked with for seven years. I'm not sure just what happened, but he quickly lost his objectivity and began to work against me.

It took a lot of offers and counter-offers to come to an agreement. They insisted that even though I was to be paid off by December, they would not be able to mail the check until December 31. Only later did I learn that this delay made me liable for one-half of our earnings for the entire year—even though I had only received my earnings through to June. I ended up paying $50,000 in taxes. I was so angry I couldn't sleep for days. I felt totally betrayed by my friend and the accountant. I felt they had conspired to crush me.

I really had to reach deep to forgive that one, but I somehow found the strength to do so. Then I realized that I needed to write and ask their forgiveness, too. I felt such a release as I licked the envelope and put the letter in the mail. No matter what the answer, I needed to be free of my anger.

About a month later, a friend of mine who had advised me to forgive called to ask if I had been able to do so. I told her that I had, and she answered, "I thought so; *I thought so; I've noticed a real freeing in him, too.*"[5]

FORGIVENESS SETS ME FREE

"And his lord was wroth, and delivered him to the tormentors" (Matt. 18:34 KJV). "Torturers" is the Greek translation, not tormentors or jailers. In ancient times some of the tortures applied to imprisoned debtors were dragging about heavy chains, undergoing a near-starvation diet, being forced to do excessive labor. "This is how my heavenly Father will treat each of you unless you forgive your brother from your heart" (v. 35). When we refuse to forgive, God throws us into prison and hands us over to the torturers. Harsh words. Nobody can say for sure what or who our torturers are, but it doesn't sound as if it's worth holding a grudge over. I do know this, the most tortured soul in the church is the person who clings to anger, resentment, and unforgiveness. He is bound.

The Spirit is quenched; prayer is dull; worship is destroyed. Nothing he does can please God. The person's songs of praise are nauseating to Him; his prayers are met with closed ears; and his own cries for forgiveness are ignored.

But forgiveness changes all that. When I forgive, I no longer feel that I am dragging heavy chains behind me; my starved soul is nourished by His grace; His yoke is no longer a burden, but a blessing. I can once again sing with the congregation of the righteous.

CHAPTER 14

THE COST OF FORGIVENESS

Forgiveness isn't cheap.

Nor is it easy.

It certainly wasn't easy or cheap for Christ. In the Garden of Gethsemane, He said to His disciples, "My soul is overwhelmed with sorrow to the point of death" (Matt. 26:38). Then He prayed, "My Father, if it is possible, may this cup be taken from me. Yet not as I will, but as you will" (Matt. 26:39). As Jesus looked into the cup, He was repulsed, for it contained all the filthy rags of self-righteousness and unrighteousness of mankind, past, present, and future. Naturally He shrank back from drinking that cup.

Think of all the heartbreak and inhumanity and injustice you see portrayed on your TV screen. That's just today's cup. Then add to it thousands of years of that same heartbreak, inhumanity, and injustice—all in that cup. What a bitter cup! He who had never known sin was actually to become sin itself, and He who had known blissful fellowship with the Father from eternity would cry out in a few hours, "My God, why have you forsaken me?" (Matt. 27:46).

But thank God, He also prayed, "My Father, if it is not possible for this cup to be taken away unless I drink it, may your will be done" (Matt. 26:42).

That was the only way. Drink the cup, endure the shame and pain of the Cross—only then could forgiveness be procured. Let us never lose the wonder: Christ died for us that we might be forgiven. I often give myself a test: if I can read Isaiah 53 and not be moved, I know my heart is cold. Back in the seventies, revival fire was burning across our country. Three of us were going around holding conferences on revival. Thousands attended, some driving hundreds of miles. Each preacher had his specialty. One would preach on the Spirit-filled life, another on faith. My specialty was prayer and intercession.

One evening before the service, God and I had a wrestling match. He was leading me to preach on the suffering servant of Isaiah 53; I wanted to preach on my specialty. I remember saying to myself: *They can hear about Christ's death in their own churches. They've driven hundreds of miles to hear me speak on prayer and intercession. What's the use of them coming all this distance to hear something they can hear in their own churches?* No sooner were those arrogant thoughts thought than God smote me. *You are in bad shape,* He seemed to say, *if you think the story of the Cross is boring!*

I preached on Isaiah 53. In heaven, we'll not be discussing our sermons on prayer and faith and the Holy Spirit; we will be worshiping the Lamb who was slain. Forgiveness could not be obtained without death. And death is involved in every act of forgiveness. What is the cost of forgiveness?

DEATH

Death. "Then He said to them all, 'If anyone choose to be my disciple, he must say "No" to self, put the cross on his shoulders daily and continue to follow me'" (Luke 9:23 WILLIAMS). Say no to self. Does your self ever talk to you? Make suggestions? Issue demands? Mine does. Its words fill my brain like air fills a balloon. It says things like, "Don't let her get by with that!" or "Blow your horn! Louder!" or "Look out for number one."

We must learn to say no to self and yes to Christ. And notice that we are to take up our cross daily, for daily we need to die to self so we can live unto Christ. This is how we make real Paul's words to the Galatians: "I have been crucified with Christ and I no longer live, but Christ lives in me. The life I live in the body, I live by faith in the Son of God, who loved me and gave himself for me" (Gal. 2:20).

Excuse me, there's someone ringing my doorbell. I'll look out the peephole to see who it is. Can't be too careful these days. Oh, I recognize three former companions: anger, bitterness, and resentment.

"Yes, who are you looking for?"

"Ron Dunn. We're old friends. He'll be glad to see us."

"He doesn't live here anymore."

"What happened?"

"He died."

"Well, who lives here now? We'll see anybody."

"Jesus Christ."

Excuse me for the interruption. Funny, when I mentioned that Christ lives here, they fled. Oh, well, where was I?

Dying to self means dying to our selfish feeling, our right to be angry, our right to revenge. I read of a man who insisted on his right to hate. I don't know him but I'd not count on his forgiveness if I wronged him.

We hear a lot about rights today. People want, *demand*, their rights, and if necessary, they will sue to get them. Have you noticed lately all the newspaper accounts of underage children suing their parents for their rights? I don't know whether you realize it or not, but when you surrendered yourself to the lordship of Christ, you gave up all your rights. A Christian has only one right, and that is to do the will of God. Listen, we don't even have a right to our own lives because we have been bought with a price: "Do you not know that your body is a temple of the Holy Spirit, who is in you, whom you have received from God? *You are not your own*; you were bought at a price. Therefore honor God with your body" (1 Cor. 6:19–20, emphasis added).

SILENCE

Some people pride themselves on saying whatever they think. But that's not necessarily something to be proud of. We are not obliged to say whatever we think, no matter if it is the truth. Sometimes the wisest and holiest thing we can do is keep our mouths shut. James told us, "We all stumble in many ways. If anyone is never at fault in what he says, he is a perfect man, able to keep his whole body in check . . . Consider what a great forest is set on fire by a small spark. The tongue also is a fire, a world of evil among the parts of the body. It corrupts the whole person, sets the whole course of his life on fire, and is itself set on fire by hell" (James 3:2, 6). The uncontrolled tongue has split more churches, broken more hearts, and divided more homes than anything I know of.

"Where no wood is, there the fire goeth out; so where there is no talebearer, the strife ceaseth" (Prov. 26:20 KJV). One thing is certain, if there is strife in our fellowship, there is a talebearer among us. The Hebrew word translated "tale-bearer" means "whisperer," painting a vivid picture of the method of the talebearer.

Bonhoeffer says, "Thus it must be a decisive rule of every Christian fellowship that each individual is prohibited from saying much that occurs to him. This prohibition does not include the personal word of advice and guidance . . . But to speak about a brother covertly is forbidden, even under the cloak of help and good will; for it is precisely in this guise that the spirit of hatred among brothers always creeps in when it is seeking to create mischief."[1]

James had another word (I'm not sure I would have liked James; he could put a damper on a fellowship dinner!): "Brothers, do not slander one another. Anyone who speaks against his brother or judges him speaks against the law and judges it. When you judge the law, you are not keeping it, but sitting in judgment on it. There is only one Lawgiver and Judge, the one who is able to save and destroy. But you—who are you to judge your neighbor?" (James 4:11–12).

"Hey, wait just a minute!" someone says. "You ought to be telling that to the guy who wounded me!" You're right. But if we don't forgive, we will end up committing the same crime as he. So I'm speaking to the spear-throwers as much as I am to the wounded. Both Saul and David need to hear this.

So "do not let any unwholesome talk come out of your mouths, but only what is helpful for building others up according to their needs, that it may benefit those who listen" (Eph. 4:29). For many of us, following this exhortation would keep us quiet for years.

MEEKNESS

Our culture considers meekness weakness. But while he was alive, Moses was the meekest man in all the earth, and I certainly wouldn't call him weak. Jesus was meek, but in no way was He weak. What is meekness? Paul described it: "Do nothing out of selfish ambition or vain conceit, but in humility consider others better than yourselves. Each of you should look not only to your own interests, but also to the interests of others. Your attitude should be the same as that of Christ Jesus" (Phil. 2:3–5). This attitude is to be a deliberate effort and preference. Paul was able to say such things because he considered himself the greatest sinner of all (1 Tim. 1:15). Of course, this is terrible psychology and would never be curriculum for a "Building Self-Esteem" class.

I have many favorite hymns, one being, "Jesus, I My Cross Have Taken," written by Henry Francis Lyte. The first verse goes like this:

> Jesus, I my cross have taken,
> All to leave and follow Thee;
> Destitute, despised, forsaken,
> Thou from hence my all shall be:
> Perish every fond ambition,
> All I've sought or hoped or known;
> Yet how rich is my condition,
> God and heav'n are still my own!

A few years ago my denomination revised the hymn book and took that one out. I asked a member of the committee why they removed it. "Poor psychology," he said. "Bad for self-esteem." I guess that's why they also changed the words of "At the Cross" from "such a worm as I" to "sinners such as I"? Gotta make man look good.

But the higher we think of ourselves, the more prone we are to judge others for failing to measure up to our standards. In reality, many of us are not nearly as concerned with folks becoming like Jesus as we are that they become like us. Paul warned us of thinking of ourselves more highly than we ought (Rom. 12:3). Thomas à Kempis said, "Never think that thou hast made any progress at all till thou look upon thyself as inferior to all."

PATIENCE AND LONG-SUFFERING

For the Colossians, Paul prayed that they might be "strengthened with all might, according to his glorious power, unto all patience and longsuffering with joyfulness" (Col. 1:11 KJV). Paul piled up words to emphasize his point. He said literally "that you might be continually (as a habit of life) empowered with all kinds of power, according to His glorious power (the level of the resources available)." But the key word in these verses is *unto*, to what purpose. What would God have me do that would require all that power? Preach to stadium-filled crowds, heal the sick, raise the dead, or move mountains? No—to be *patient* and *long-suffering*. Isn't that amazing?

The easiest thing I do in the Christian life is to preach. I figure that if I could preach twenty-four hours a day, seven days a week, my sin count would drop to its lowest point. The hardest thing I do is to be patient and long-suffering.

These two words are interesting. *Patience* means "endurance under adverse circumstances." Peter O'Brien says that it "signifies that kind of perseverance which enables one to hold the position already taken in battle against enemy attacks from without."[2] *Long-suffering* means "being patient with people without getting even." It is self-restraint that does not retaliate a wrong.

So patience has to do with adverse circumstances, and

long-suffering with offensive people. Being patient and being long-suffering are two of the most difficult qualities to acquire in the Christian character. We need the full measure of God's glorious power to achieve them.

Perhaps you can think of more things it costs to forgive. Perhaps you think that these are too high a price to pay. But the cost of forgiveness is not nearly as high as the cost of unforgiveness.

CHAPTER 15

THE ACT OF
FORGIVING

If I am forgiven, I must forgive.

I must forgive to be forgiven.

"But if you do not forgive, neither will your Father in heaven forgive your trespasses" (Mark 11:26 NKJV). We've met those words before in Matthew 6:15 at the conclusion of the Model Prayer. Jesus means that if there is unforgiveness toward another in my heart while I am praying for forgiveness, I am unrepentant and rebellious, and God won't hear my prayer for forgiveness or anything else. More than anything else, unforgiveness erects a stone wall that blocks our path to power in prayer.

Our Lord's statement comes at the end of a tremendous promise. Let's review the story. One day as Jesus and His disciples were leaving Bethany, Jesus was hungry. In the distance He saw a fig tree covered with leaves and went over to it to see if it had any fruit: "When he reached it, he found nothing but leaves, because it was not the season for figs. Then he said to the tree, 'May no one ever eat fruit from you again.' And his disciples heard him say it" (Mark 11:12–14).

Now wait a minute. Wasn't that cruel and unfair punishment to curse a tree because it bore no fruit out of season? Surely the tree was not at fault. But Jesus was giving His disciples an object lesson. The little tag the Holy Spirit added to Jesus' words—"and his disciples heard him say it"—tells us something far deeper was involved than the mere cursing of a fig tree.

It was not yet the season for figs, but the tree was covered with leaves. Those fig trees bore fruit and leaves simultaneously, so that if a tree bore leaves, you had a right to expect fruit on it. But that particular tree was a nothing-but-leaves tree. By its leaves (and it must have been a bumper crop because Jesus saw them from a long distance), it was professing fruit, but it was a false profession. The tree was a hypocrite. The reference, of course, was to Israel, who had all the leaves of religion but none of the fruit of righteousness.

The next morning they passed the fig tree. Overnight it had withered from its roots and died. When Peter saw it, he said, "Rabbi, look! The fig tree you cursed has withered!" (v. 21). I guess he thought Jesus would be surprised too. But Jesus calmly said, "Have faith in God . . . I tell you the truth, if anyone says to this mountain, 'Go, throw yourself into the sea,' and does not doubt in his heart but believes that what he says will happen, it will be done for him. Therefore I tell you, whatever you ask for in prayer, believe that you have received it, and it will be yours. And when you stand praying, if you hold anything against anyone, forgive him, so that your Father in heaven may forgive you your sins" (Mark 11:22–25).

Notice the chain-link fence in this passage. First, Jesus promised us that, through faith, we can move mountains. Then He said, "Therefore," linking what He had just said to what He was about to say concerning prayer. Then He said, "And when you stand praying," forgive. One verse can't be taken in isolation; they all go together—and the bottom line is forgiveness. An outline will help our understanding:

1. Jesus promises us power to remove mountains.
2. This mountain-moving power is released by faith.
3. This faith is expressed in prayer.
4. This prayer is conditioned by forgiveness.

If I don't forgive, I can't pray; if I can't pray, I can't express my faith; if I can't exercise my faith, the mountain will not move. Got any mountains you can't move? You've prayed, you've believed, you've fasted, you've rebuked the devil— you've done everything, yet nothing changes. Perhaps you, too, need to look under the rock in your heart and see if there is a worm of unforgiveness hiding there. Ah, there's the culprit.

In the early seventies, our church experienced a great revival, a supernatural awakening, an extraordinary outpouring of the Spirit we had never before witnessed. Although our attendance increased and many people were saved, the outstanding feature of that revival was confession and forgiveness of sin. Not among lost people, but among the members of the church. For hours one after another would stand and confess bad attitudes and resentment and bitterness, asking for the church's forgiveness. And the forgiveness was always granted. I didn't ask the people to do that. There was no urging or manipulation on my part. It was the work of the Holy Spirit. I remember one service that was delayed in starting because a woman bolted out of her seat and cried, "I can't be in this service without first asking the church's forgiveness for my backbiting!"

Throughout the years of my ministry, I have tried to be a student of revival and spiritual awakenings. One thing I have learned: every revival that I read about began with confession and forgiveness among God's people. If we are to exercise the power God has given us, there must be forgiveness.

THIS FORGIVENESS IS UNILATERAL

Me, myself, and I must forgive. Whether the offender repents or not, I forgive. Even if the offender doesn't know he has offended me, I forgive. I don't have to say a word to him; I just forgive.

By the way, Jesus didn't tell us to go to that person and say, "I forgive you." Only if he knows there is something between the two of you do you need to tell that person you forgive him.

Years ago, I was at a conference, and a young woman, whom I didn't know, came up to me and said, "Pastor Dunn, I want you to forgive me." Never having met this person, I couldn't imagine what she had done to need my forgiveness. So I asked, "Why? What for?"

"Because I have never liked you," she said.

I told her I forgave her, and to this day I wonder what it was about me that she didn't like. Since I didn't know she had something against me, it wasn't necessary to tell me. All she needed to do was to forgive me for whatever it was about me she didn't like. She actually created another problem. I had to forgive her for not liking me!

Sometimes forgiveness can be only unilateral. A woman told me that she had finally forgiven her father for the way he had treated her as a child. The father had been dead twenty years.

THIS FORGIVENESS IS ALL-INCLUSIVE

Two words: *anything* and *anyone. Anything,* Jesus said. No matter how dark the deed, how terrible the betrayal, how deep the wound, forgive. You say I don't understand how terrible the thing was the person did? Was it worse than nailing God's Son to a tree? Your sins—and mine—put Him there. Nothing anyone has done against us can be compared to what we have done against God.

Anyone. No matter how unlikable or unrepentant he is, you must forgive.

"While we were yet sinners, Christ died for us" (Rom. 5:8 KJV). If you're serious about forgiveness, try this exercise. Get a piece of paper (legal size may be necessary), and at the top, write on the left side, "Anyone," and on the right side, write, "Anything." Underneath the headings list everyone and everything you have a grudge against. Then draw a line through each one, saying, "Lord, I forgive this." Remember, forgiveness is a decision, not an emotion.

THIS FORGIVENESS IS UNCONDITIONAL

Catherine Marshall admitted, "For years I attached a condition to my forgiveness; if the other person saw the error of his ways, was properly sorry, and admitted his guilt, then—yes, as a Christian, I was obligated to forgive him. Finally, I had to face the fact that this was *my* pat set of conditions, not Christ's."[1]

Forgive. "But," you say, "you don't know what he did to me." Oh, I must have misread the passage. Did Jesus say, "Forgive if what the other person did wasn't really bad"? Hey, if people knew the whole truth about us, they wouldn't treat us half as well as they do. Dietrich Bonhoeffer asked, "What does it matter if I suffer injustice? Would I have deserved even worse punishment from God, if He had not dealt with me according to His mercy?"[2]

"But he will do it again," you protest. Oh, did Jesus say, "Forgive if the person promises never to do it again"? I'm glad God doesn't make that condition.

"But if I forgive him, he will get by with it," you say. Oh, did Jesus say, "First get even, then forgive"? Of course, this is our real concern—that others will get by with what they have done. When it comes to offenses against ourselves, we have an exaggerated sense of justice. But part of forgiveness is giving up our demands for revenge and trusting that God alone, to whom vengeance belongs, will see that justice is done.

"Well, I would forgive him, but I can't forget what he did," you say. Oh, did Jesus say, "Forgive and forget"? No. But I hear that a lot, don't you? "You must forgive and forget." I have never found this phrase in the Bible. God is the only One who has the ability to forget. He remembers our sins against us no more—forever. God can do that, but we cannot. Actually the best way to remember something is to try to forget it. Every time you remember the offense, remember also that you have forgiven it.

"Okay, I will forgive him if he comes to me and says he is sorry," you say. "And don't give me any of that 'Oh, did Jesus say . . .' stuff. After all, God didn't forgive me till I came to Him and repented. So I'm only making the same condition that God did."

Oh, didn't I read somewhere that Christ was the Lamb slain from the foundation of the world (Rev. 13:8)? And that we were chosen in Him before the creation of the world (Eph. 1:4)? And didn't Paul say, "You see, at just the right time, when we were still powerless, Christ died for the ungodly . . . But God demonstrates his own love for us in this: While we were still sinners, Christ died for us" (Rom. 5:6, 8)? The only reason we were able to come to God in the first place is that God in Christ had already provided forgiveness for sins.

TEARING UP OUR IOUS

Get your ledger. You have one. So do I. Everyone does. You may not know you have one, but you do, and you carry it with you everywhere you go. It's called "Accounts Receivable," and in it you keep a record of everything bad that happens to you. It is the record of the IOUs you're holding against others. The entries read something like this: "The pastor didn't speak to me this morning; he owes me an apology." "The Hoopers didn't invite me to their Christmas party; they owe me an apology." Sound familiar? I thought it would. Forgiveness involves gathering up all the IOUs you're holding against people and tearing them up. They are no longer in your debt. They owe you nothing—not amends, not an apology, nothing. Forgiveness means that all debts have been paid in full.

Do it. Do it now. Tear them up. You might just find that mountain in your life sliding into the sea.

CHAPTER 16

GETTING EVEN GOD'S WAY

When I was a child, our family went on a vacation, driving from Arkansas to Minnesota. I don't remember much about the trip, but I have a vivid memory of a place we visited in Missouri. At the mouth of a stone cave there was a beautiful pond of sparkling deep blue water. I was leaning over the little rock wall surrounding it, peering into its depths, when I heard the guide say, "We've never found a rope long enough to touch the bottom." I immediately backed away in fear. What a moment ago was a thing of beauty to me was now an object of terror. If I fell in there, they would never find me.

Revenge reminds me of that dark blue pool. For a moment it looks attractive, luring us in with a promise of satisfaction. But if we fall into it, it has no bottom, and we may never get out. A Chinese proverb says, "Whoever opts for revenge should dig two graves." The urge to retaliate just increases our enemy's power over us. Someone has said that revenge is like an acid that does more harm to the vessel in which it is stored than to the person on which it is poured.

Or instead of revenge, we can hide ourselves behind a wall of self-protection, shutting ourselves off from anything and anybody that might hurt us. Forrest Church observed, "Self-protection seems user-friendly, yet all it does is close us off from others. Self-protection veils our hearts. Even more sadly, it may armor them."[1]

But the thirst for revenge, like the Missouri pond, runs deep in the human heart. We live in a "get even" society. Road rage is real, exemplified by two bumper stickers I saw. One said, "Honk, if you've never seen an Uzi fired from a car window." A pickup truck wore this badge of honor: "Keep honking—I'm re-loading." Under the guise of defending our honor, we have kicked heads, smashed faces, broken noses, punched stomachs, and shot to death those who offended us. We live in a violent, vigilante society.

There is a better way—the way of Jesus. We might call this the final step in surviving friendly fire. It is learning to live with our enemies or, more accurately, learning to *love* our enemies: "You have heard that it was said, 'You shall love your neighbor and hate your enemy.' But I say to you, love your enemies, bless those who curse you, do good to those who hate you, and pray for those who spitefully use you and persecute you" (Matt. 5:43–44 NKJV).

Love your enemies! Impossible; or at least it sounds impossible. But Jesus would not have commanded it had we been unable to do it. I said in a previous book[2] that every command is a promise because God will not ask us to do something without imparting to us the power to obey that command. Jesus said to Lazarus, "Come forth." That's asking quite a lot from a dead man. If Lazarus could have come forth, he would have done so before then. An impossible command. But Lazarus did come forth because Jesus imparted to him the power to come forth. And if Jesus commands us to love our enemies, there is a way to do it.

The question is not, *Can* we love our enemies, but *Will* we? Again, it's not an emotion; it's a decision. It is a decision of the will, not an exercise in willpower. And there's a big difference between the will and willpower. The Christian life is lived in the realm of the will, not willpower. Unfortunately, many Christians believe it is a matter of willpower, of determined resolution. To illustrate this point, consider the following story.

I remember something that happened in gym class when I was a young teenager in junior high school. I don't remember what it was exactly, but when the coach was calling the roll, I probably said something smart, trying to be funny (my elementary school teacher always told me my mouth would get me in trouble). But the coaches back then didn't have a sense of humor, and this coach put me in a corner of the gym and told me to stay there the whole hour with my arms outstretched sideways at shoulder height. I thought, *Is that the best you can do?* I could easily handle that punishment. So I stood in the corner as he commanded. As time went by my ache intensified and my muscles burned. I lowered them just a smidgen. "Dunn!" the coach yelled. I immediately regained height. But it got harder and harder. Oh, did I mention I was holding a broom in each hand? Finally my willpower gave way and so did my arms. I discovered something stronger than willpower; it's called the power of gravity.

And there is something stronger than your willpower—the power of the flesh. The secret is not in willpower, but in the power of the will: I choose to obey God.

WHY LOVE OUR ENEMIES?

Two things are true about us and our enemies that should compel us to love them:

1. We share a common grace. Why should we love our enemies? Because God does. Loving our enemies, Jesus said, was showing ourselves to be the children of God, "for He makes His sun rise on the evil and on the good, and sends rain on the just and on the unjust" (Matt. 5:45 NKJV). Now I wouldn't do that, would you? If I were God, I would freeze them by taking away their sun and burn their crops by withholding rain. Of course, if I were God, I wouldn't love you or me either. But Christ died for us while we were still sinners. The point that Jesus was making was that you can't tell God's enemies from His friends by the way He treats them. Luke told us that He is "kind to the ungrateful and wicked" (Luke 6:35). Refusing to love our enemies is tantamount to denying that such a God exists. The God of the Bible is the God not only of His friends but also of His enemies. He is not only our God, but also the God of those who have wronged us.

2. *We share a common guilt.* Listen to Jesus' words about judging: "Why do you look at the speck of sawdust in your brother's eye and pay no attention to the plank in your own eye?" (Matt. 7:3). Well, there must be something wrong— there just may be a splinter in my eye, but the log is in my enemy's eye. Doesn't Jesus understand the situation? Evidently not, for He continued: "How can you say to your brother, 'Let me take the speck out of your eye,' when all the time there is a plank in your own eye? You hypocrite, first take the plank out of your own eye, and then you will see clearly to remove the speck from your brother's eye" (Matt. 7:4–5). Now wait just a minute. Is Jesus calling me a hypocrite because I, being without sin, am judging another brother's sin? Sounds that way. Also sounds as if He is saying you can't see clearly either. With that log in your eye you can see nothing objectively.

I guess I don't know Jesus as well as I thought I did. I was certain He would take my side in this conflict, but instead He is telling me I have no right to judge anybody—unless I want God to judge me for my sins. No, thank you. I would appreciate God's forgiving and forgetting the log in my eye. And He will—if I forgive the splinter in my brother's eye. As Paul reminded us, "Who are you to judge someone else's servant? To his own master he stands or falls" (Rom. 14:4).

Walter Wink offers an interesting insight: "The 'splinter' in the other's eye is a chip off the same log that is in one's

179

own eye."[3] He proposes this exercise: name an enemy and list all the things you dislike about that person, or persons. Then go through that list and ask yourself how many of those same characteristics are true of you.[4]

Ouch. I tried it and wasn't pleased with my findings. But isn't this true of all of us? I loved my father, but there were a few small characteristics that irritated the fool out of me. Now grown, I find myself doing the same things, or so Kaye tells me. And I hear the same from many other adults. It's uncanny how often we end up with the same habits we really disliked in our parents.

And so, Wink observes, our enemies may bring us a gift: "To see aspects of ourselves that we cannot discover any other way than through our enemies . . . The enemy is thus not merely a hurdle to be leaped on the way to God. The enemy *can be* the way to God."[5] While we are trying to change our enemies, God may use them to change us.

SO HOW DO WE DO IT?

We love our enemies by treating them the same way God treats them, letting our sun shine on them and our rain fall on them. *We treat them as though they were our best friends.* Others ought not to be able to distinguish between our friends and our enemies by the way we treat them.

Jesus said that we are to pray for them. "Oh, I will. I will pray fire and brimstone down on them," you say. You know that's not what Jesus meant. He meant that we should pray blessings, not brimstone, on them. And I'll promise you this: you cannot for long pray blessings for your enemy, and that person remain your enemy. We are to do good to those who persecute us. Bake them a cake or give them your tickets for the football game or, better still, invite them to go with you. "But what if they throw the cake in my face? What if they tear up the tickets?" Again, you are not responsible for their responses. By offering, you have obeyed the command: "If it is possible, as far as it depends on you, live at peace with everyone" (Rom. 12:18).

Remember, the goal of God's creation and redemption was that man might live in fellowship with God and with man. The old creation failed and so we have the new creation, which at times doesn't seem to fare much better. But it was for this unity that Jesus prayed. Three times in the High Priestly Prayer, John 17, Jesus asked this for His followers:

Holy Father, protect them by the power of your name—the name you gave me—*so that they may be one, as we are one.* (v. 11, emphasis added)

That all of them *may be one,* Father, just as you are in me and I am in you. May they also be in us that the world may believe that you have sent me. (v. 21, emphasis added)

I have given them the glory that you gave me, *that they may be one as we are one:* I in them and you in me. May they be brought to *complete unity* to let the world know that you sent me and have loved them even as you have loved me. (vv. 22–23, emphasis added)

Notice the standard of this unity: "as we are one." Can you imagine jealousy or division in the Godhead? We are to be one, even as Jesus and His Father are one.

Notice the reason: "that the world may believe that you have sent me." The most ignorant sinner knows that unity should be the mark of believers. But a divided fellowship will never convince the world that Jesus is the Christ sent from God.

So our God-given goal is unity. Unity doesn't mean union. Some have used these verses as justification for doing away with all denominations and joining together. But union and unity aren't the same. You can take two tomcats, tie their tails together, and throw them over a clothesline, and you've got union—but not unity.

Nor does unity mean uniformity, that we must all think and act and dress alike. We retain our individuality within unity.

Unity? What is it? I think I can best explain it by taking you back to those old World War II movies about the Battle of Britain. At night when the German bombers flew over London, giant searchlights began probing the skies. Finally one spotlight would find an enemy bomber. Immediately all the other searchlights in that area would train their powerful beams on the same plane to give the antiaircraft gunners a better target. At least, that's how they did it in the movies.

182

And Christian unity is training our hearts and minds on one thing. Despite our differences, we focus on one thing, the main thing: Jesus Christ, magnified and glorified in the black skies of this lost, warring world.

We love our enemies because God loves them. We love our enemies because they need to be loved. We love our enemies because *we* need to be loved. We love our enemies because the world needs to know that Jesus is the Savior of the world.

A CLOSING WORD

This is all I know about surviving friendly fire. Is it enough? I hope so. I think so. The alternative is to become a spear-thrower. If that is our intent, we should remind ourselves of how Saul summed up his life: "Behold, I have played the fool" (1 Sam. 26:21 KJV).

NOTES

PROLOGUE

1. *Time*, 25 April 1994 (from its Internet site).
2. Lewis B. Smedes, *Forgive and Forget* (San Francisco: Harper & Row, 1984), ix, 13.
3. Philip Yancey, *What's So Amazing About Grace?* (Grand Rapids: Zondervan, 1997), 11.

CHAPTER 1

1. Stephen L. Carter, *Integrity* (San Francisco: Basic Books, 1996), 7.
2. William Barclay, *The Gospel of Matthew*, vol. 1 of *The Daily Study Bible* (Philadelphia: Westminster Press, 1956), 101.
3. Gertrude Himmelfarb, *The De-Moralization of Society* (New York: Knopf, 1995), 10–11.
4. Ibid., 13.
5. L. Gregory Jones, *Embodying Forgiveness* (Grand Rapids: Eerdmans, 1995), 61.
6. Dietrich Bonhoeffer, *Life Together* (San Francisco: HarperCollins, 1954), 30.
7. Larry Crabb, *Connecting* (Nashville: Word, 1997), xvii.

CHAPTER 2

1. John R. W. Stott, *Guard the Gospel* (Downers Grove, IL: InterVarsity Press, 1973), 119.
2. "How Firm a Foundation," an early American hymn by John Rippon (1787).

CHAPTER 3

1. *Sunday Daily Oklahoman,* 22 June 1997.
2. David G. Brenner, *Healing Emotional Wounds* (Grand Rapids: Baker, 1990), 15–16.
3. James Q. Wilson, *The Moral Sense* (New York: Free Press, 1993), 55.
4. Walter Wangerin Jr., *Little Lamb, Who Made Thee?* (Grand Rapids: Zondervan, 1993), 117.
5. John Bowlby, *Attachment,* 2d. ed. (San Francisco: Basic Books, 1982), 177.
6. Monica McGoldrich, *You Can Go Home Again* (New York: Norton, 1995), 24.
7. Hope Edelman, *Motherless Daughters* (Reading, MA: Addison-Wesley, 1994), 112.
8. David Blankenhorn, *Fatherless America* (San Francisco: Basic Books, 1995), 1.
9. See Elizabeth Loftus and Katherine Ketcham's *The Myth of Repressed Memory,* published by St. Martin's Griffin, and *Making Monsters* by Richard Ofshe and Ethan Watters, published by Charles Scribner's Sons.

CHAPTER 4

1. Rollo May, *Psychology and the Human Dilemma* (New York: Norton, 1979), 25.
2. Eric Fromm, *To Have or to Be* (New York: Bantam, 1981), 96–97.

NOTES

CHAPTER 8

1. Richard Keyes, "The Idol Factory," in *No God But God*, ed. Os Guinness and John Seal (Chicago: Moody Press, 1992), 29.
2. Ibid., 32–33.
3. Stephen Charnock, *The Existence and Attributes of God* (Grand Rapids: Baker, 1979), quoted by Dr. Robert Norris during a lecture at Reformed Theological Seminary.
4. Keyes, "The Idol Factory," 33.
5. Neil Clark Warren, *Finding Contentment* (Nashville: Thomas Nelson, 1997), 3.
6. Alexander Souter, *A Pocket Lexicon of the Greek New Testament* (Oxford: Clarendon Press, 1957), 163.

CHAPTER 9

1. John Flavel, *The Mystery of Providence* (Edinburgh: Banner of Truth Trust, 1995), 22.
2. Louis Berkhof, *Systematic Theology* (Edinburgh: Banner of Truth Trust, 1976), 166.
3. Charnock, *The Existence and Attributes of God.*
4. R. C. Sproul, *The Invisible Hand* (Dallas: Word, 1996), 17.
5. Westminster Confession of Faith, Chapter 5, "Of Providence," part 1.
6. Flavel, *Mystery of Providence*, 18, emphasis added.
7. William Plummer, *Jehovah-Jireh: A Treatise on Providence* (Harrisonburg, VA: Sprinkle Publications, 1997), 25.

CHAPTER 10

1. Earl D. Radmacher, *You and Your Thoughts* (Wheaton, IL: Tyndale, 1977), 41.
2. Flavel, *Mystery of Providence*, 117.

CHAPTER 11

1. John MacArthur, *The Freedom and Power of Forgiveness* (Wheaton, IL: Crossway, 1997), 10.
2. Lewis Drummond, *What the Bible Says* (Nashville: Abingdon Press, 1975), 112.
3. Forrest Church, *Life Lines* (Boston: Beacon Press, 1996), 98.
4. MacArthur, *Freedom and Power of Forgiveness*, 10.
5. Dietrich Bonhoeffer, *Spiritual Care*, trans. J. C. Rochelle (Philadelphia: Fortress Press, 1985), 62.

CHAPTER 13

1. Yancey, *What's So Amazing About Grace?*, 88.
2. Related by L. Gregory Jones, *Embodying Forgiveness* (Grand Rapids: Eerdmans, 1995), 35–36.
3. Ibid., 39.
4. Philip Rieff, *The Triumph of the Therapeutic* (Chicago: Univ. of Chicago Press, 1967), 26.
5. Johann Christoph Arnold, *The Lost Art of Forgiveness* (Farmington, PA: Plough Publishing House, 1997), 79–80, emphasis added.

CHAPTER 14

1. Bonhoeffer, *Life Together*, 92.
2. Peter T. O'Brien, *Colossians, Philemon*, vol. 44 of Word's Biblical Commentary (Waco: Word, 1982), 24.

CHAPTER 15

1. Catherine Marshall, *Something Better* (New York: McGraw-Hill, 1974), 36.
2. Bonhoeffer, *Life Together*, 95.

CHAPTER 16

1. Church, *Life Lines*, 90.

2. *The Faith Crisis*, published in 1984 by Tyndale House, now out of print. Available in Great Britain from STL Publications, under the title *Don't Just Sit There, Have Faith.*

3. Walter Wink, *Engaging the Powers* (Philadelphia: Fortress Press, 1992), 271.

4. Ibid.

5. Ibid., 273.

ACKNOWLEDGMENTS

I'd like to acknowledge several people:

Tony Preston, whose mention of the "hand of Saul" sowed the seeds of this book.

My dear friend Michael Catt for much-appreciated material, advice, and support.

Joanne Gardner, my associate and friend for more than thirty years, who never seems to tire of ABC work (above and beyond the call of duty).

The many wounded who shared with me their stories. Thanks. Although some stories don't appear in the book, each one contributed to my belief that it needed to be written.

Stephen and Kimberly, my son and daughter, for their always expected, never disappointing support and encouragement.

And as always, my wife, Kaye, who listens with grace to me ramble, complain, and swear never to write another book. She is my most valuable critic. Even her criticism is encouraging.

ABOUT THE AUTHOR

Ronald Dunn was in ministry for more than thirty years. He began preaching at the age of fifteen, and pastored his first church at the age of seventeen. He was a graduate of Oklahoma Baptist University and earned his M.Div. at the Southwestern Baptist Theological Seminary.

In 1975, he left the pastorate to found Lifestyle Ministries, an organization that promotes conferences and produces Bible study tapes for missionaries, laypeople, and students. Dunn traveled forty weeks each year—mostly to churches—holding conferences and frequently spoke overseas. Dunn also served as an adjunct professor at two seminaries. He authored several books, including the popular *Don't Just Stand There . . . Pray Something!*

Ron passed away in 2001, leaving behind his wife, Kaye. They had two children, Stephen Mitchell and Kimberly Kaye. Their first child, Ronald Jr., died in 1975 at the age of eighteen.

For more information on Ronald Dunn and his ministry, visit his Web site at *www.rondunn.com*.